Musical Democracy

Musical Democracy

Nancy S. Love

State University of New York Press

Published by
State University of New York Press, Albany

Printed in the United States of America

For information, address State University of New York Press,
194 Washington Avenue, Suite 305, Albany, NY 12210–2384

Production by Diane Ganeles
Marketing by Michael Campochiaro

Library of Congress Cataloguing-in-Publication Data

Love, Nancy Sue, 1954–
Musical democracy / Nancy S. Love
p. cm.
Includes bibliographical references (p.) and index.
ISBN-13: 978-0-7914-6869-2 (hardcover : alk. paper)
ISBN-10: 0-7914-6869-0 (hardcover : alk. paper)
ISBN-13: 978-0-7914-6870-8 (pbk : alk. paper)
ISBN-10: 0-7914-6870-4 (pbk : alk. paper)
1. Music—Political aspects. 2. Music—Social aspects. I. Title.

ML3916.L68 2006
780'.0321—dc22

2005033340

10 9 8 7 6 5 4 3 2 1

. . . Most people don't seem to realize that there are still thousands on thousands of folks that go more by singing than they do by reading. (Woody Guthrie, quoted in Denisoff, *Sing a Song of Social Significance* 1983, 102)

Contents

Acknowledgments

A number of colleagues have provided comments on earlier versions of my arguments here. I am especially grateful to Mary Caputi, Fred Dallmayr, Thomas Dumm, Kathy Ferguson, Dennis Fischman, Mary Hawkesworth, Mark Mattern, John Nelson, Shane Phelan, Morton Schoolman, Stephen Schneck, Tracy Strong, and Stephen White. A spring 2000 sabbatical leave from Pennsylvania State University allowed me to begin serious work on this project. I also want to thank the following Penn State graduate students who provided research assistance for the manuscript: Sushmita Chatterjee, Margaret Farrar, Chad Lavin, Challen Nicklen, and Jamie Warner. My thanks as well to Penn State undergraduates Alaine Day and Anthony Inverso, who located many of my source materials.

I could not have asked for a better editor than Michael Rinella at the State University of New York Press. I especially want to thank him for seeing the value of a novel approach to political theorizing and selecting two anonymous reviewers whose comments have made this a better book. I also want to thank Diane Ganeles for supervising the production process and Pat Hadley-Miller for copyediting the manuscript. My thanks as well to Sue Poremba for proofreading the manuscript and Carol Inskip for preparing the index.

I would like to thank the original publishers for permission to reprint material from several earlier publications. Portions of chapter two were previously published in "Disembodying Democracy: Gendered Discourse in Habermas's Legalistic Turn" in *Confronting Mass Democracy and Indus-*

trial Technology: German Political and Social Thought from Nietzsche to Habermas, ed., John McCormick (Durham: Duke University Press, 2002), 321–342. Chapters three and four, respectively, are revised versions of the following articles: "Rawlsian Harmonies: Overlapping Consensus [as] Symphony Orchestra," *Theory, Culture, & Society* 2003, vol. 20(6): 121–140 and "'Singing For Our Lives': Women's Music and Democratic Politics," *Hypatia: A Journal of Feminist Philosophy* 17:4 (Fall 2002): 71–94.

In an interview with Wendy Kupferman, Holly Near said "I need you, the people out there doing this work, to pass this music on. It can do an amazing amount of work on its own if it gets out there" (2000, 35). I write from the conviction that books also carry this power to work on their own in the world. As I wrote this book about the capacity of music to move people, I struggled with a severe injury that has limited my mobility. When it seemed too difficult to work, I drew inspiration from another author who wrote through illness, a woman I have never met, Laura Hillenbrand. I read *Seabiscuit*, watched the movie, held onto the lesson "better to break a man's [or woman's] leg than his heart"—and continued to write. It is to her that I dedicate this book.

CHAPTER ONE

Music and Democracy

> To come to terms with the turns taken in and by our arguments, . . .we often must re-cognize, re-poeticize, even re-animate them. We must re-turn the motion to our figures. (John S. Nelson, *Tropes of Politics: Science, Theory, Rhetoric, Action* 1998, 28)

Concert, dissonance, harmony, and, by analogy, chorus, orchestra, symphony—philosophers often employ musical metaphors to describe political processes. National anthems, military marches, and protest songs—music also marks many political events. However, music is seldom included in the repertoire of *political* communication.[1] Puzzled by this omission, I began to explore various relationships between music and politics. What associations between them are suggested by these musical metaphors? Why do all existing societies have their traditional forms of music? Why is music also so prominent in the political activism of social movements? How does music contribute to processes of identity formation and community building? Does it facilitate understanding between individuals? Across cultures? Beyond language? How does it work to sustain political cultures and promote political change? Most important, how might musical practices further our understanding of democratic politics?

Three larger concerns motivate this series of questions. Each involves a false opposition or, at least, an overdrawn one, which limits mainstream concepts of politics. The first is the distinction between reason and rhetoric or, more narrowly, philosophy and poetry. Understood as empty eloquence, mere style or, worse, manipulative speech, rhetoric is often opposed to the rigors of formal, deductive, logical, systematic, etc., argument. This opposition is part of a larger one between humanistic and scientific methods of inquiry. In his *Tropes of Politics, Science, Theory, Rhetoric, Action*, John Nelson defines rhetoric broadly as "a concern with what is communicated, how, by, and for whom; to what effect; under what circumstances; and with which alternatives" (1998, xv). He argues that rhetorical studies are no substitute for logical analyses, but instead augment them. Since the argumentative style of any discipline is intended to persuade its chosen audience, hypotheses and data have meaning only in a rhetorical context. Like literary arts, philosophical logic, and scientific inquiry employ culturally-specific rhetorical styles. Studies of their rhetoric acknowledge the aesthetic and political context—the community of language and power—within which their arguments succeed or fail. Rhetoric persuades audiences by adapting to established conventions, following set traditions, and, when necessary, creating new meanings. Attention to rhetoric promotes the reflective interpretation and creative expansion of language and, with it, human knowledge. Nelson writes: "rhetoric of political inquiry should strive to improve research and action by teaching people engaged in studying or practicing politics to learn from their own inquiries. Especially they should learn how their rationality and inquiry are thoroughly rhetorical, truly tropal, intensely political" (1998, 33).

Nelson's approach to understanding rhetoric owes more to critical theory, broadly defined to include deconstruction, genealogy, hermeneutics, and phenomenology, than to game-theoretic analyses of strategic action. He is more concerned with how societies create meanings than with how politicians win—or lose—arguments and elections (Nelson 1998, 9). This orientation, one that I share, distinguishes "rhetoric" from what William Riker defines as "heresthetics." Heresthetics is the "manipulation of the structure of tastes and alternatives within which decisions are made, both the objective structure and the structure as it appears to participants. It is the study of the *strategy* of decision" (1983, 55). For Riker, rhetoric is a subset of heresthetics. Heresthetics structures the political context within which rhetorical strategies are used to persuade adversaries (1983, 61). Political scientists and, more specifically, social movement scholars, have long studied a version of what Riker calls "heresthetics" under the rubrics of political culture (Almond and Verba 1980, 1989). However, this approach to rhetoric arguably relegates culture to a mere frame for the real activity of movements, which is politics (Eyerman and Jamison 1998, chapter 1; Tarrow 1998, introduction). I focus instead on how rhetoric links cultural expression with political action by constructing interpretive communities, by forming, sustaining, and transforming individual and collective identities. This is a process of *reproducing* politics, a process of symbolic action, including symbolic domination and symbolic protest (Eyerman and Jamison 1998; Lee 1998; Melucci 1996).

The tropes that interest me most here are metaphors and their cognates, similes. The Greek root of metaphor is *metapherein,* which means to bear or to carry from one place to another. It suggests a transfer of meanings from one context to another (Miller 1979, 156). In "Four Master Tropes," Kenneth Burke defines metaphor as "a device for seeing something *in terms* of something else" (1969, 503). He proposes "perspective" or "point of view" as appropriate synonyms: "metaphor tells us something about one character as considered from the point of view of another character. And to consider A from the point of view of B is, of course, to use B as a *perspective* upon A." The transfer of meaning in metaphor illuminates some aspects of "A" and simultaneously minimizes others. It also involves some incongruity, since similarity is not the sole basis for comparison. Metaphors do their work by creating new associations, by invoking available meanings that previously went unacknowledged (Johnson 1981, 24). As a result, when a metaphor is translated into literal language some loss of meaning will inevitably occur.

According to Lakoff and Johnson, "any adequate theory must explain both how metaphors are grounded in the common experience within a culture and how new metaphors can alter the conceptual system in terms of which we experience and talk about our world" (1999, 33). They argue that metaphors should be understood as both cognitive and cultural. As cognitive structures, metaphors are primordial, cross-cultural, expressions of human beings' embodied consciousness. The transfer of meaning characteristic of these primary metaphors is a conflation of sensory and subjective experience, a result of an infant's inability to distinguish self and other. Lakoff and Johnson write: "From a conceptual point of view, primary metaphors are cross-domain mappings, from a source domain (the sensorimotor domain) to a target domain (the domain of subjective experience) preserving inference and sometimes preserving lexical representation" (1999, 58). Some examples of primary metaphors are "more is up" or "close is warm" or "knowing is seeing" and, I argue, "voice is music." Where embodied experience is similar, primary metaphors are likely to be shared constructs, even to take universal forms. However, these conceptual metaphors employ a variety of culturally-specific linguistic referents. Basic concepts have multiple logics and with them "multiple metaphorical structurings" (Lakoff and Johnson 1999). In this sense, metaphors are not only an embodied cognition, but also an imaginative rationality (Lakoff and Johnson 1999). For example, in American politics, liberals and conservatives construe "Government as Parent," but they vary in whether it is (or should be) a "Nurturant Parent" or "Strict Father," respectively. These different metaphors guide their thinking about a variety of moral and political issues (Lakoff 2002). Yet, the metaphors involved in their reasoning processes are often so unconscious that they appear to be common sense. As Nelson argues, over time "our" tropes begin to seem literal or even right, hence, the need arises to re-turn to them (1998, 29).

This brings me to a second false opposition, between aggregative, deliberative, and more recently, agonistic democracy. Political theorists have long distinguished two basic types of democracy: aggregative and deliberative.[2] Aggregative democrats describe a politics of instrumental reason, private interests, competitive elections, representative officials, and institutional/ized power. Deliberative democracy instead directly involves citizens in public discourse about political issues, a process that ideally enlarges their perspectives and produces consensual decisions. Deliberative theorists today have largely conceded the dominance of aggregative politics in modern western states. They are focused on developing more inclusive communication within existing political institutions (elections, courts, and legislatures) and extending deliberative processes to private interactions (economic and familial). In deliberative democratic theory, new social movements complement aggregative organizations, like interest groups, lobbying firms, and political parties, as vehicles for political participation. Social movements not only work to influence politico-economic institutions, but also help to give politics the "sense of meaning" that sustains a vital civil society.

Among critics of deliberative democracy, a third theory is increasingly prominent: agonistic democracy (Connolly 1999; Bickford 1996; Brown 1995; Honig 1993). Agonistic democrats affirm what William Connolly calls the "politics of becoming" or "that conflictual process by which new identities are propelled into being by moving the preexisting shape of diversity, justice, and legitimacy" (1999, 10). Social movements, Connolly argues, not only deploy established identities to engage political institutions, they also embody "fugitive currents of energies and possibility exceeding the cultural fund of identities and differences. . . ." (1999, 143). Working with these micropolitical energies, they alter perceptions at a subliminal level and change the shape, even preclude the option, of politics-as-usual. Ideally, they promote forms of "self-artistry," including "relational arts," which continually reinvoke "the plurovocity of being" (Connolly 1999, 7). Connolly describes the potential result as a democratic politics characterized by "a deep pluralism nourished by a generous ethos of engagement" (1999, 130).

Democratic theorists of all three types use vocal metaphors, but they do so in different ways.[3] Aggregative democrats describe a visually-based politics of viewpoints and perspectives, symmetry and reciprocity—of mirrors and mirroring (Young 1997, 50). A "logic of identity" operates here, which requires that representatives "substitute" or "stand-in" for their constituents (Young 2000, 123). The "voice" of the people is quickly translated into votes cast, limited to counting "ayes" or "nays" (Verba, Schlozman, and Brady 1995; Flammang 1997). Deliberative theorists tend instead to translate voice into speech and, more narrowly, argument. As their critics note, the deliberative ideal of rational argument can privilege the communication style of middle-class white men and marginalize women and other minorities (Young 2000). It may also reflect the origins of modern western democracy in a literary public sphere (Landes 1995). According to Walter Ong (1991), the transition from oral to literate societies introduced a world of visually represented verbal material. Sound or, more precisely, sound/ing, a moving material force, became letters and words, objects separate(d) from their contexts. The early bourgeois public was a "reading public," adept at "text formed thought," including "abstract categorization," "formally logical reasoning processes," and "articulated self-analysis" (1991, 55, 74, 82). As I discuss later, deliberative democrats' emphasis on rational argument reinforces Ong's distinction between orality and literacy (Biakolo 1999; Boyarin 1992; Hudson 1994).[4] Like aggregative democrats, they tend to translate vocal expressions into a visually-based symbolic structure.

However, recently deliberative democrats have begun to pluralize forms of political communication. Iris Young (1997) argues for what she calls a "communicative democracy," which supplements rational argument with greeting, rhetoric, and storytelling. These practices "recognize the embodiment and particularity of interlocutors" and provide "ways of speaking across difference in the absence of significant shared understandings" (1997, 69).[5] For Young, "Public communication . . . also includes politicized art and culture—film, theater, song, and story—intended to influence a wider public to understand the society or some of its members in particular and often different ways" (2000,

168). Yet artistic and cultural expressions that "reclaim" group identities do not necessarily qualify as political discourse (2000, 104). Young maintains that "primary claims of justice . . . refer to experiences of structural inequality more than cultural difference" (2000, 105).[6]

By separating cultural from political communication, Young sustains—even as she loosens—the connections between rational argument and political discourse. In a different context, Nancy Fraser challenges democratic theorists who limit struggles for justice to redistributive politics. She argues that

> economic injustice and cultural injustice are usually interimbricated so as to reinforce each other dialectically. Cultural norms that are unfairly biased against some are institutionalized in the state and the economy; meanwhile, economic disadvantage impedes equal participation in the making of culture, in public spheres, and in everyday life. The result is often a vicious circle of cultural and economic subordination. (1997, 15)

Fraser does not specifically discuss the implications of this "redistribution/recognition dilemma" for forms of political communication. In his recent proposal for "discursive democracy," John Dryzek suggests how they might intersect (2000). Like Young, Dryzek regards rhetoric as part of political discourse and stresses its importance for communication across cultural boundaries. However, for Dryzek, cross-cultural communication occurs not only between distinct subcultures in the public sphere, but also between those subcultures and state institutions that have their own political culture (2000, 167–168). Dryzek shares deliberative democrats' concern that public officials will use their political positions to develop rhetorical strategies that manipulate citizens emotionally. To counter this tendency, he stipulates that the various rhetorics of democratic politics must meet the same criteria as rational arguments: they must be noncoercive and connect particular interests with general interests.

Although deliberative democrats' efforts to create a more inclusive discourse are significant, they remain focused on controlling the e/motions that move civil society and, hence, limited to verbal communication. According to Dunn and Jones, "human vocality encompasses all the voice's manifestations (for example, speaking, singing, crying, and laughing), each of which is invested with social meanings not wholly determined by linguistic content" (1994, 1). Agonistic democrats extend vocal metaphors further, beyond spoken words to moving sounds. The sounds of embodied voices form a part of, what Connolly calls, the "visceral register" of inter/subjective experience (1999, 3). Visceral responses are extralinguistic, "thought-imbued intensities," which prompt disgust and revulsion and inspire ritual and symbol (1999, 29). Triggered by the amygdala, a primitive brain nodule, and stored in the hippocampus, a cranial site of primal memories, these responses often bypass more complex body/brain/culture networks and relays. In *Neuropolitics, Thinking, Culture, Speed* (2002) Connolly explores how cinema, in particular, combines image, voice, sound, rhythm, and music to work its effects at multiple—affective, cognitive, and physical—levels of viewers' experience. Culture, he suggests, is many layered, and politics, including democracy, unpredictably mobile. For agonistic democrats, like Connolly, "artful-selves" and "experimenting constituencies" are two—subjective and intersubjective—sides of a "politics of becoming" (1999, 149). Social movements continually shift back and forth, up and down, using the energies of a visceral politics as resources to move institutional politics forward in the pursuit of justice.

In *Justice and the Politics of Difference*, Iris Young suggests why aggregative and deliberative democrats might restrict or minimize the role of this visceral level of politics (1990, 131–132). Following Anthony Giddens, she argues that interactions between subjects occur on three related levels: discursive consciousness, practical consciousness, and a "basic security system" or "ontological integrity." Although the first two levels are largely conscious, the third level engages psychological deep structures. Young claims that most forms of oppression have now receded from discursive consciousness, and that they are receding from practical consciousness. However, unconscious motivations continue to manifest themselves in group-specific languages, including distinctions between so-called rational and affective or corporeal aspects of communication. Political theorists have to a great extent neglected these subconscious and/or unconscious forms of oppression. Young writes:

> A conception of justice that starts from the concept of oppression must break with such a limitation of moral and political judgment to discursively conscious and intended action. If unconscious reactions, habits, and stereotypes reproduce the oppression of some groups, then they should be judged unjust, and therefore should be changed. (1990, 150)

She proposes extending moral judgment to "habitual interactions, bodily reactions, unthinking speech, feelings, and symbolic associations" (1990, 150). At this deepest level oppression is enacted through a "body aesthetic" (1990, 149).

To recognize nonverbal communication as a form of rhetoric, even an aspect of political discourse, is to challenge a third overdrawn distinction, the opposition between aesthetics and politics. Early articulations of deliberative democracy claimed that it "draws no bright line between political speech and other sorts of expression" (Cohen 1989, 30). Yet Cohen distinguishes "non-political expressions" from "the deliberative conception [which] construes politics as aiming in part at the formation of preferences and convictions, not just at their articulation and aggregation" (1989, 29). Gutmann and Thompson also discuss rhetorical appeals as precursors to deliberative politics: "Nondeliberative means may be necessary to achieve deliberative ends" (1996, 134). Even Dryzek earlier stated that "there are . . . domains of life where discursive democracy does not belong. Communicative rationality finds its grounding in the linguistic interaction of collective life. It does not speak to theater, wit, religion, music, visual arts, play, poetry, or private experience, unless of course those activities enter into the constitution of collective choices" (1990, 220). Regarding new social movements, Dryzek suggests that "the description new *political* movements would be more appropriate, though it is probably too late for such renaming to stick" (1990, 49).

Deliberative democrats' attempts to contain cultural politics, especially more embodied discourses, reflect their fears of an aestheticized politics. These fears may be well-founded. George Kateb writes of "the power of an unaware and unrationalized aestheticism to move people to act immorally with an apparent innocence" (2000, 6). Yet he admits that aesthetic cravings are unavoidably human. We seek satisfaction for our senses, our imaginations, in the pursuit of beauty, itself part of a larger search for meaning. Kateb writes: "Aestheticism" is "the effort to get from experience (let me clumsily call it non-art) what persons ordinarily seek and often find in works of art—high, low, or middling. Art should be the site where the most intense aesthetic satisfactions are found" (2000, 12). When "social reality" becomes the primary site of aesthetic experience, these cravings are all too often either ignored and/or manipulated. Kateb distinguishes a proper aesthetic attitude —one of distanced, detached observation—from the cravings inadequately satisfied by an aestheticized politics. The proper attitude can, he claims, contribute to a "democratic aestheticism" or a "receptivity or responsiveness to as much of the world as possible—its persons, its events and situations, its conditions, its patterns and sequences" (2000, 31). This democratic aestheticism is self-conscious and self-controlled; it does not trump morality, but instead serves it.

If public discourse is inevitably rhetorical, the issue becomes how—not whether—aesthetics and politics are related. Although a "democratic aestheticism" may initially seem compelling, I argue that the tension Kateb identifies between aesthetics, ethics, and politics itself presumes a specific body aesthetic.[7] It replicates deliberative democrats' inattention to what Orville Lee calls processes of symbolic domination. Lee understands civil society as a symbolic order that constitutes individual and collective identity. Social categories are institutionalized and materialized both in the dominant discourse—a "public of letters"—and in the cultural practices of counter-publics. As Lee puts it,

> It is important . . . to see the impact of the constitutive force of the symbolic order as *two-sided*. This symbolic force both *constrains* (i.e., constitutes and disciplines) the range of meanings attached to social categories (and the *social bodies* they reference) and *enables* symbolic practices (i.e., the political and institutional claims made on the basis of social categories) which affirm or contest the existing range of meanings. (1998, 444)

Lee defends a concept of "symbolic protest," which challenges not only deliberative democrats' commitment to rational argument, but also Kateb's conscious, controlled aesthetic judgment. Both presume that power relations do not penetrate our very notions of democratic discourse. By privileging rational argument, deliberative democrats practice what Kateb calls an "unconscious aestheticism." They separate proper procedures for democratic legitimacy from the pursuit of social justice, and permit the former to delimit the latter. However, democratic discourse is only legitimate when it includes the voices of all citizens, and such inclusivity requires pluralizing the styles as well as the topics of communication (Young 2000).

"Voice as music," I argue, provides an especially productive site for promoting a more inclusive democratic discourse. Song lyrics frequently represent political views even as they express cultural identities. More important, as moving sound, music blurs and crosses, defines and expands relationships between self and other, challenging established identities and institutions. In a passage worth quoting at length, Simon Frith describes this process:

> In taking pleasure from black or gay or female music I don't thus identify as black or gay or female . . . but,

> rather, *participate in imagined forms of democracy and desire,* imagined forms of the social and the sexual. And what makes music special in this familiar cultural process is that musical identity is both fantastic—idealizing not just oneself but also the social world one inhabits—and real: it is enacted in activity. Music making and music listening, that is to say, are bodily matters; they involve what one might call *social movements*. In this respect, musical pleasure is not derived from fantasy—it is not mediated by daydreams—but is experienced directly: music gives us a real experience of what the ideal could be. (1996, 74)

The aesthetic ideal Frith expresses here may include "beauty," but this is not its crucial feature. More important is what Jean Harrell calls "profundity." According to Harrell, musical rhythms and sounds often evoke primal experiences shared cross-culturally. "Profundity" is "rooted in a rudimentary recall . . . recognition of an intrinsic value in the biological fact of life established previsually, therefore probably prenatally" (1992, 20–21). I will argue that music avoids the dangers of essentialism, since its moving sounds bridge the various dualisms on which essentialized differences depend (Frith 1996). This is true whether profundity is understood in biological/cultural, neurological/psychological, or material/spiritual terms. However, profundity is not an aesthetic criterion that enables us to discriminate between disciplinary and emancipatory music or, in Kateb's terms, between democratic music and more suspect forms.

Earlier I mentioned Dryzek's stipulation that democratic rhetorics must satisfy the same standards of noncoercion and generalizability as so-called rational arguments. Orville Lee provides more extensive criteria for determining whether symbolic practices meet democratic standards of inclusivity. Moving beyond Kateb's formal aesthetic, he suggests three substantive criteria for making judgments about aesthetic creations: 1) "the quality of knowledge about the symbolic order that they bring into existence"; 2) "their contribution to de-hierarchization of existing symbolic categories"; 3) "the types of less coercive and less hierarchical symbolic interactions that they bring into the repertoire of symbolic practices" (1998, 450). The musical metaphors and practices I consider in later chapters meet these criteria in different ways and to varying extents. More important in the present context, they suggest that Kateb's distinction between aesthetic cravings and a democratic aestheticism may itself constitute a form of symbolic domination, an attempt to control corporeal aspects of aesthetic experience.

Having troubled often overdrawn distinctions between aesthetics and politics, types of democracy, and reason and rhetoric, I now return to my opening question: How might musical practices further our understanding of democratic politics? In the following chapters, I explore music as metaphor and model for democratic politics. I first consider how Jürgen Habermas and John Rawls employ musical metaphors—voice and symphony, respectively—to express the sense of justice that animates their discourse ideals. In chapter two, I argue that Habermas's vocal metaphors reveal both the motivating force and the cultural limits of his deliberative democracy. For Habermas, mutual understanding is best enabled by purely linguistic and, hence, rational, communication. He describes the rationalization-cum-linguistification of society as a transition from sacred to secular, primitive to modern, and oral to literate, worldviews. Since the rational subjects and critical publics of western democracy originated in literary reading rooms, salons, and coffeehouses, it is no surprise that his public discourse follows a textually-based form, that is, rational argument. As political actors, citizens learn to translate their existential and/or subcultural experiences into claims for legal rights. Habermas's vocal metaphors reveal how much is lost when embodied voices assume generalized form as public text. By displacing voice/s, he reveals a deeper commitment, which limits his deliberative democracy: the desire to resolve differences into harmony.

In chapter three, I argue that Rawls's political liberalism provides a musical structure for the resolution of differences that deliberative democrats so often seek. Like Habermas, Rawls relies on intuitive ideas of a liberal political culture to support the principles of justice chosen by his democratic citizens. Rawls draws his concept of their well-ordered society—a social union of social unions—from Wilhelm von Humboldt, a seldom-noticed source. Paralleling von Humboldt's use of musical metaphors, Rawls depicts overlapping consensus as a symphony orchestra. With its three-part movement from harmonic stability (exposition) through instability (development) again to stability (recapitulation), the symphony has been described as a musical *Bildungsroman.* Whether conducted by Adam Smith's invisible hand or Arturo Toscanini's legendary baton, the orchestra reconciles individual freedom with social responsibility. Although a shared sense of justice moves Rawls's citizens, they play a formal, instrumental, and, some argue, a highly-rationalized and textually-based music. I conclude by comparing two symphonies, a UNESCO-funded system of youth orchestras in South America dedicated to civic education through classical music, and the more democratic ethos of "PauWau: A Gathering of Nations," by the indigenous composer, Brent Michael Davids.

Unlike symphonic form, which to a great extent mirrors liberal justice, the music of social movements reveals and releases new energies from a resonant civil society. I turn to musical practices of the feminist and civil rights movements as models for a more radical democracy. In chapter four, I examine how lesbian-feminist music (euphemistically, "women's music") exemplifies the transformative power of vocal sound. I emphasize the music of Holly Near, political artist, cultural worker, and founder of Redwood Records. With her music, Near pushes the boundaries of linguistic consciousness and, with it, political discourse. She describes music as "poet's code," as a way "to speak the truth without saying the words" (1985, 76). When Near, an out-lesbian, sings heterosexual love songs she unsettles established identities. She also promotes the formation of coalitions between the members of her diverse audiences. Her performances engage listeners as participants and encourage a responsive and responsible citizenry. Near's feminist commitments—non-essentialism, consciousness-raising, empowerment, and coalition-work—are familiar ones. What is new is their musical meaning as sound in motion. When injustices originate in a body or, more precisely, an anti-body aesthetic, "women's music" that taps into the e/motions of civil society can promote democratic change.

The body aesthetic of Western reason associates oppressed groups more closely with spiritual and/or material forces, and it stigmatizes both as premodern, regressive, and primitive. Simply put, modern, secular, Western, public discourse lacks soul (Caraway 1991). In chapter five, I explore how civil rights music or freedom songs simultaneously express the horrors of racial slavery and the spirit of democratic community. My focus is the cultural politics of Sweet Honey in the Rock, an a cappella ensemble of five African-American women, based in Washington, DC, founded by Bernice Johnson Reagon, one of the original SNCC Freedom Singers. Moving beyond (white) feminist claims that "the personal is political," Reagon writes, "I think everything is political. We are about being accountable" (quoted in Caraway 1991, 178). African-American song traditions exemplify what Martin Luther King called the "soul-force" of democracy. When leaders "raise a song" they invite others to take it up, to assume responsibility for their actions, to participate in the living history of a people. This call-and-response mode combines individuality and community, spontaneity and structure, and mirrors radical democratic processes. These features of African-American singing open up the self, creating a more expansive individual. To paraphrase Cordell Reagon, music changes individuals, who can then change governments (quoted in Seeger and Reiser 1989, 85).

In chapter six, I return to the relationships between music and democracy and, more broadly, aesthetics and politics, with which I began. Habermas and Rawls, I argue, fail to fully realize the democratic potential expressed in their own musical metaphors. They confine embodied voices to the spaces of private life and individual autonomy—the liberal boundaries of democratic politics. The sounds of citizens' voices enter their public discourse only after translation into a public text, at best, animated by "symphonic justice." Musical practices of the feminist and civil-rights movements model a more radical, one might say, a more musical democracy. Drawing on the insights of activist musicians, I conclude by outlining some of its crucial features. Most important, the musical democracy, whose features I describe, promotes the ongoing creation of expansive individuals, citizens capable of performing democracy in public spaces open to any and all expressions of voice.

CHAPTER TWO

Habermas's Voices: Rationalizing Resonance

> Each system should play its own melody but with a new rhythm. (Jürgen Habermas, *Between Facts and Norms: Contributions to a Discourse Theory of Law and Democracy* 1996, 344)

> The currents of public communication are channeled by mass media and flow through different publics that develop informally inside associations. Taken together, they form a "wild" complex that resists organization as a whole. (Jürgen Habermas, *Between Facts and Norms: Contributions to a Discourse Theory of Law and Democracy* 1996, 307)

In his 1969 tribute to Adorno, Habermas writes:

> Adorno never accepted the alternatives of remaining childlike or growing up; he wanted neither to put up with infantilism nor to pay the cost of a rigid defense against regression, even were it to be "in the service of the I." In him there remained vivid a stratum of earlier experiences and attitudes. This sounding board reacted hypersensitively to a resistant reality, revealing the harsh, cutting, wounding dimensions of reality itself. (1985a, 104)

Although Habermas values Adorno's "primordial subjectivity" and his "enchanting analyses," he clearly aligns himself with what he regards as a more mature, modern, and rational world view (Morris 2001; Schoolman 2001). Habermas's metaphors associate Adorno—personally, philosophically, and politically—with musical experience, in particular, with the dangers of a romanticized nature and an aestheticized politics. Unlike Adorno and other first-generation critical theorists for whom aesthetic experience sustained hopes of an emancipatory reconciliation between individual and society, Habermas turns away from "aesthetically informed philosophy" when he develops his theory of communicative rationality (Duvenage 2003, 1).[1] Compared to his former teacher, Habermas is described as "having no music in his soul."[2]

Habermas's unwavering commitment to rational communication offers some support for this characterization of his philosophy. Even the violent symbolic power of the 9/11 terrorist attacks could not shake his faith in the efficacy of reasonable argument. In a recent interview, Habermas attributes the causes of terrorism to "distortions in communication" (2003, 35). Yet Habermas's early works give literary culture a major role in the creation of the public sphere and, with it, the formation of democratic publics. It is his later writings that confine aesthetic experience to a smaller space, the private realm of expressive individuality (Leet 2004). There his defense of communicative rationality from colonization by politico-economic systems overshadows aesthetic concerns.

In this chapter, I argue that aesthetics and, more specifically, music, continue to animate the deepest levels of Habermas's deliberative democratic theory. Echoing Adorno, Habermas describes his idealized citizens as the "sounding boards" of a "resonant" and "vibrant" civil society. When their voices "resound" in the public sphere, they guide Habermas's theory of communicative rationality toward a more radical vision of democracy.

Reason vs. Rhetoric?

> . . . the tools of rhetoric are subordinated to the discipline of a *distinct* form of argumentation. (Habermas, *The Philosophical Discourse of Modernity* 1987b, 209–210)

In his theory of communicative action, Habermas distinguishes reason from rhetoric, a distinction he associates with another between "problem-solving" and "world-disclosive" language (White 1991). For Habermas, ordinary language coordinates our everyday activities and, along with the relevant expert discourses, identifies and implements solutions to problems. Literary works and, more generally, artistic performances, enhance, heighten, and reveal latent meanings already present in ordinary speech. However, these aesthetic creations also "bracket," "disempower," or "neutralize" the problem-solving functions of everyday language. Habermas describes the result: "Neutralizing their binding force releases the disempowered illocutionary acts from the pressure to decide proper to everyday communicative practice, removes them from the sphere of usual discourse, and thereby empowers them for the playful creation of new worlds—or, rather, for the pure demonstration of the world-disclosing force of innovative linguistic expressions" (1987b, 201). Habermas maintains that artistic creations have the capacity to disclose new worlds precisely because they can detach themselves from the problems of everyday life.

Although Habermas usually sustains his distinction between "world-disclosive" and "problem-solving" language, he does occasionally suggest that it resembles a continuum more than a dichotomy (1985b, 1987b, 2002).[3] In a seldom-noted discussion of Mary Pratt's theory of "literary speech acts," Habermas recognizes the numerous fictional, metaphorical, narrative, and rhetorical elements in so-called "normal" language (1985b, 390). Indeed, Pratt may present a greater challenge to Habermas's theory of communicative rationality than he acknowledges. Pratt argues that claims to linguistic autonomy not only deny the illocutionary force of literary works, but also impoverish ordinary language. To separate rhetoric from reason, as Habermas does, "misrepresents the status of literary discourse in the grammar as completely as it misrepresents the role of aesthetic considerations in our speech behaviour outside literature" (1977, 16). Pratt instead maintains that literary and nonliterary language develop in similar contexts and have similar purposes. She sees interactions between authors and readers, speakers and listeners, as specific examples of a more general performer/audience relationship. All of these relationships involve asymmetrical or, at least, asynchronous, expectations, obligations, and rights. For example, participants in conversation take turns in different roles, among them, speaking clearly and listening carefully, remaining silent or asking questions. Their interactive performances follow shared rhetorical norms that enable them to have meaningful exchanges.

When Habermas, albeit reluctantly, acknowledges rhetorical aspects of everyday speech, he also concedes the importance of metaphorical language. He writes, "We are now well aware, since Mary Hesse at the latest, that even the language of the sciences is shot through with metaphors; this is plainly true of the language of philosophy, which can never of course be entirely absorbed into its role as a stand-in for scientific theories with strong universal claims" (1986, 161). For Hesse, metaphors involve a transfer of meaning between two referential systems: a primary object is described or explained using a word associated with a secondary one, for example, "man is a wolf." By transferring meanings between systems, metaphors ". . . select, emphasize, or suppress features of the primary; new slants on the primary are illuminated; the primary is 'seen through' the frame of the secondary" (1966, 163).[4] Hesse maintains that metaphors—like literal language—are meant to communicate and, hence, they follow linguistic rules of intelligibility (1966, 165). They also exhibit a kind of rationality in the latent meanings and unconventional associations they disclose. According to Hesse, metaphors need not be "true": "they will, however, be rational, because rationality consists just in the continuous adaptation of our language to our continually expanding world, and metaphor is one of the chief means by which this is accomplished" (1966, 176).

Habermas's passing remarks on Pratt and Hesse moderate his opposition to the aestheticizing of language and, with it, politics. Since communication is unavoidably rhetorical, the issue becomes the appropriate relationship between ordinary speech and expert discourses, including philosophy and literature (Duvenage 2003). According to Habermas, everyday life and expert cultures "live off (*leben von*)" the power of metaphors to illuminate experience by "altering modes of perception," by "expanding" and "enriching" meanings (1985c, 415; 1987b, 209). However, a tension emerges here with wide-reaching implications for Habermas's theory of democratic discourse. To perform its "world-disclosive" functions aesthetic experience requires some autonomy from other aspects of society, especially the pervasive influence of mass culture. Creative artists and art critics must have the freedom to express their subjective experiences of "'artistic truth,' aesthetic harmony, exemplary validity, innovative force, and authenticity" (1987b, 207). Yet artistic creations must nonetheless prove their utility for the larger society.

Habermas attempts to resolve this tension by making philosophy "trump" over aesthetics. In modern highly differentiated societies, philosophical thinking represents the interests of the lifeworld in creating shared meanings among the various forms of communicative action (1998, 383–401). Habermas's critique of rhetoric is best understood in this broader philosophical context. Having conceded a role for rhetoric, he still wants to distinguish appropriate linguistic styles from valid philosophical arguments. He presents rhetoric as a "premodern" and "prelinguistic" aspect of language; it relies on custom, myth, and ritual, more than reason. In modern societies, rhetoric is often mobilized in the service of "tradition" or even "ideology" (Eyerman and Jamison 1998). For Habermas, this means that the rhetoric of arguments is primarily strategic; it is a device used to manipulate, persuade, and, hence, coerce, interlocutors. For this reason, rhetoric seldom fosters mutual understanding and often contributes to distortions in communication.

Habermas concludes that rhetorical strategies and their effects should be carefully controlled. Expert cultures must "cleanse (*reinigen*)" and "tame (*zahmen*)" their rhetoric, making it a "tool (*das Mittel*)" suitable for rational communication (1987b, 190, 209–210). When asked whether stylistic concerns are a diversion and regression in philosophical arguments, Habermas responds that his rhetoric changes with his purposes (1986, 161–162). He also maintains that "Significant critics and great philosophers are noted writers" (1987b, 209). Rhetoric, his metaphors suggest, is an impure and unruly form of language. By implication, philosophers should limit their metaphors and choose them with great care.

Given their paucity, Habermas's metaphors may be even more significant than he acknowledges. His call for a philosophically controlled rhetoric suggests that metaphors merely substitute for literal language. However, Hesse's interactive approach to metaphors better suits their "world-disclosive" functions, which Habermas also acknowledges. If metaphors reveal unacknowledged assumptions of a shared lifeworld, they may be examples of what Habermas calls *a posteriori* universals. These universals are the products of socialization processes, unlike the *a priori* universals that Habermas claims exist prior to society. He identifies two types of *a posteriori* universals: 1) perceptual/motivational universals are fields of meaning, which develop from human beings shared "neuro-physiological sense organization"; 2) cultural universals express the intersubjective contexts or "socio-cultural backgrounds"—the interpretations and institutions—that give word systems their substantive meanings (1970b, 364–365).[5] The latter include word systems that all cultures share, but which take varied forms, for example, kinship words or color words. In important respects, these features of Habermas's theory prefigure current analyses of metaphor as an "imaginative," "embodied," "affective" rationality (Lakoff and Johnson 1999, chapter 1). They also anticipate recent theories of politics, including the politics of identity, as animated by a visceral register of psychosomatic responses (Connolly 1999; 2002).

Perceptual/motivational and cultural universals remain relatively unexamined components of Habermas's theory of rational communication. However, they are important substantive complements to his better-known—formal or procedural—dialogue-constitutive universals. They are also crucial categories for his project of radical democracy, which requires mutual understanding across cultural differences. Indeed, an analysis of Habermas's major metaphors should illuminate his rhetorical context, highlight culturally-specific aspects of his philosophical discourse, and perhaps even disclose new possibilities for pluralizing democratic communication.

Habermas's Communicative Rationality

> Participants in argumentation have to assume in general that the structure of their communication, by virtue of features that can be described in purely formal terms, excludes all force. . . . (Habermas, *The Theory of Communicative Action* 1987a, 25)

To distinguish reason from rhetoric Habermas posits an idealized language community, itself an extrapolation from what he regards as "idealizations inhabiting language itself. . . ." (1996, 17). In his early theory of communicative competence, Habermas derives the preconditions for rational communication from the generalized features of speech acts, not the specific characteristics of any particular language. Competent speakers must not only use *their* language properly, but also employ a set of "dialogue-constitutive universals." The most important of these universals are the personal pronouns, "I" and "You," "He" and "They," which allow speakers to "assume incompatible [dialogue] roles simultaneously" or to see themselves as their interlocutors see them (1970b, 370). Speakers demonstrate their communicative competence by mastery or, at least, approximation, of an ideal speech situation. Habermas defines the conditions of ideal speech as intersubjective symmetry "in the distribution of assertion and dispute, revelation and concealment, prescription and conformity, among the partners of communication" (1970b, 371). In other words, anyone can put any issue on the agenda and everyone agrees to give reasons for their claims. All participants speak openly and sincerely regarding their individual positions and any decisions that are made apply equally to all. These conditions potentially free communication from power by allowing only the "forceless force of the better argument" to prevail (1984, 25).

Habermas has consistently acknowledged the idealizations involved here. The speech situation he proposes presumes "an exclusively linguistic organization of speech and interaction," (1970b, 369), itself based on his distinction between "pure dialogue-constitutive universals" and "non-linguistic means of communication, e.g., gestures and contexts" (1970b, 367, 369). At the required level of abstraction, Habermas's citizens speak the same language or, more precisely, they use language in the same ways and with the same meanings. They also presumably have equal access to the prerequisites for effective communication, including education and employment. In his early writings, Habermas defends ideal speech with quasitranscendental arguments about moral-cognitive development, specifically the progressive evolution of humanity from an ape-like "*language* of gestures and a system of *signal calls*" to purely "linguistic communication" (1979b, 139–140). His later theory of communicative rationality rests instead on a reconstruction of the "rationality potential" inherent in human speech.

According to Habermas, a society is rationalized "to the extent that it permits interactions that are not guided by normatively *ascribed* agreement but—directly or indirectly—by communicatively *achieved* understanding" (1984, 340). In premodern societies, lifeworld traditions are neither the background context for public discourse nor its primary subject; instead, they have the "*bonding*," "*compelling*," and "*spellbinding*," authority of "the sacred" (1996, 24). Sacred authority conflates inner and outer worlds, precludes rational arguments about validity claims, and is, for those very reasons, "prelinguistic." When the latent rationality of communication is "unfettered"—released and developed—the realm of the sacred gradually "shrinks": mythical powers become transcendent gods and, later, universal norms (1987a, 88). Ironically, religious practices inaugurate this process of linguistification that eventually overtakes them. They form a "we" of faith and ritual analogous to the "syntactical relationship" between "I" and "Thou," whose locus eventually shifts from sacred to secular community (Habermas 2002, 23).

With the rationalization of society, "language takes over the functions of achieving understanding, coordinating action, and socializing individuals and thus becomes the medium through which cultural reproduction, social integration, and socialization take place" (1987a, 288). In modern societies, competent speakers learn to differentiate between three "formal worlds": nature, society, and self. They also learn to use distinct criteria to assert, justify, and evaluate validity claims about these different aspects of their society. They ask: Are statements about objective conditions true? Are actions right given social norms? And, are individuals expressing themselves sincerely? (1984, 335–336).

According to Habermas, the rationalization-cum-linguistification of communication creates the possibility of mutual understanding between different cultures. Although meanings are never context-independent, in modern societies neither are they context-dependent. Habermas argues that his theory of communicative rationality reveals "*general* contextual conditions" competent speakers must meet in order to be understood cross-culturally (1984, 335–336). When speakers present arguments on behalf of their validity claims, they "presuppose a world that is identical for *all possible* observers, or a world intersubjectively shared *by members*, and they do so in an abstract form freed of all specific content. Such claims call for the rational response of a partner in communication" (1984, 50). Communicative rationality potentially enables mutual understanding, but it cannot reunify modern societies. The differentiation of society into formally distinct worlds cannot be reversed. At its best, rational communication creates "bridges" between currently "existing norms and personal identities" and a "ritually preserved fund of social solidarity" (1987a, 77). Since processes of identity formation are both subjective and intersubjective, meaningful speech acts are simultaneously "expressive" and "integrative." As I discuss in later chapters, social movements participate in this process of constructing/affirming shared meanings when they "break silence" on an issue, bringing concerns that were private or, at least, privatized, to public discourse (Habermas 2002, 61–62).

Habermas's Rational Society

> . . . the new conflicts are not ignited by distribution problems but by questions having to do with the grammar of forms of life. (Habermas, *The Theory of Communicative Action* 1987a, 392)

Habermas claims that "Only a democracy that is understood in terms of communications theory is feasible under the conditions of complex societies" (1997, 133). He offers two models—"siege" and "sluice"—to characterize the communications that occur between lifeworld traditions and politico-economic systems in modern societies. *The Theory of Communicative Action* stresses the first model of a lifeworld under siege. Here the media of political and economic systems—power and money, respectively—interact with lifeworld processes of symbolic reproduction and increasingly overwhelm them. A besieged lifeworld faces "colonization" by systems media and, in response, may either withdraw from its own traditions or sustain them in "distorted" forms. Habermas regards "cultural impoverishment" as an unfortunate and frequent result of "systemically induced reification" (1987a, 327). Critics of mass culture, he argues, often fail to perceive the potential for rational communication that persists, despite the pervasive effects of systemic rationalization. This failure limits their ability to see and support existing sources of democratic resistance. It also increases their vulnerability to irrational responses to systems domination, such as charismatic leaders and symbolic, even auratic, politics.

In contrast, Habermas maintains that an "inner logic" of lifeworld traditions, specifically, a commitment to "universal foundations of morality and law" practiced by "bourgeois socialist liberation movements," persists and reveals itself in the struggles of "progressive social movements" (1987a, 393). These movements regard the creation of meanings or, what Habermas calls, "the grammar of forms of life," as equally if not more important than the solution of problems of politico-economic redistribution (1987a, 392). Their struggles reveal the paradoxical quality of a rational/ized society: its legal system of universal rights simultaneously protects and threatens culturally specific lifeworld potentials. In a lengthy quote, Habermas outlines his political imperatives for a lifeworld under "siege":

> The point is to protect areas of life that are functionally dependent on social integration through values, norms, and consensus formation, to preserve them from falling prey to the systemic imperatives of economic and administrative subsystems growing with dynamics of their own, and to defend them from becoming converted over, through the steering medium of the law, to a principle of sociation that is, for them, dysfunctional. (1987a, 372–373)

Habermas's second model of modern society—the "sluice"—appears in his latest extension of communicative rationality to legal discourse. It further develops and modifies his notion of the relationship between a rational/ized law and lifeworld values. Like speech acts, legal orders emerge from an "*always already familiar*" lifeworld composed of meanings that they must also reproduce (1996, 22). Although Habermas once sharply distinguished lifeworld values from legal norms, he now refers to law as a "hinge" between the public sphere and political systems (1996, 56). He also increasingly includes citizens' interactions with institutional authority within the lifeworld, although he still claims language mediates lifeworld relationships, not money and power. Since the "lifeworld certainties" of modern rational/ized societies emerge from discourse, they differ significantly from the "original, auratically transfigured normative consensus" of "archaic institutions" (1996, 23). Following the secularization of government authority, "the law" acquires legitimacy only through "extensive democratization"—and not from religious sources (1996, 443). In rational/ized lifeworlds, discursively-redeemable validity claims replace faith-based "metasocial guarantees" of normative order. Lacking sacred authority, law itself is perpetually "on trial" with the democratic discourse of its citizens delivering "the verdict" (1996, 26).

According to Habermas, a tension between "objective" facts and "democratic" norms pervades all aspects of rational/ized societies, including legal constitutions (1996, 35). We have already seen its most basic form in the ongoing tension between "natural" languages and "competent" speech acts. Regarding law, this tension manifests itself in a distinction between the rights of individuals and the rights of citizens. As established fact, systems of legal rights protect the autonomy of individuals by restricting the scope of strategic action. However, legal norms are valid only when they also protect the democratic procedures by which citizens continually reauthorize them. This suggests a "conceptual or internal" relationship between democracy and law, as well as a "historically contingent" one. According to Habermas, "the democratic procedure for the production of law evidently forms the only postmetaphysical source of legitimacy" in modern societies (1996, 448). His discourse ethics, in turn, outlines acceptable discursive procedures for justifying legal norms. Indeed, when the formal rules of democratic discourse complement the formal rights of democratic constitutions, the likely result is discursively achieved—and, hence, rational—agreements among citizens on political issues.

By securing symmetrical relationships between democratic citizens as rights-bearing individuals, law also supports social solidarity, but it does so only indirectly (1996, 449). For Habermas, solidarity among the citizens of modern democracies cannot arise solely from processes of communication. Nor can it be entirely freed from the bureaucratic pressures of politico-administrative systems. Instead, the remains of a "body politic" or "popular sovereignty" are "sublimated into elusive interactions between culturally mobilized public spheres and a will-formation institutionalized according to the rule of law" (1996, 486). Habermas uses cybermetaphors to describe these interactions: the public sphere resembles a "network" where "streams of communication" are "filtered" and "bundled" into "topically specified public opinions" (1996, 360). Constituted by legal rights of individual citizens, it is further energized by diverse subcultures of civil society. In order to bring their private experiences to public expression, citizens participate in various associations, parties, and movements. Communication "flows" through these organizational "sluices" following the procedures of legal constitutionalism and, again ideally, it influences politico-economic systems (1996, 133–134). Habermas concedes that the likely result is, at best, an "eviscerated" body politic in which "structures of mutual recognition . . . preserved in the legal order, are stretched like a skin around society as a whole" (1996, 409).

As the locus of communication shifts from private to public spaces, Habermas thinks the emphasis of democratic discourse should also change. In the public sphere, politics focuses on "problem-solving" rather than "world-disclosure," and the dominant discourse is correspondingly "legal" instead of "literary." Habermas claims that citizens of modern democracies "no longer have a choice about which language they might want to use. Rather, the legal code is given to democratic subjects in advance as the only language in which they can express their autonomy" (1996, 126). Only legal discourse can extract meaning from "prelinguistic" contexts and translate it into the "specialized codes" and "organized relationships" of modern democracies (1996, 437). And, "without their translation into the complex legal code that is equally open to lifeworld and system, these messages would fall on deaf ears in media-steered spheres of action" (1996, 56).

Habermas's justification for the "sluice" model of modern democracy parallels his defense of communicative rationality: he treats legal constitutionalism as a universal/ized language. The citizens of a democracy-by-law have symmetrical individual rights that parallel—and protect—their symmetrical grammatical roles. Like democratic discourse, legal constitutions "presuppose the possibility of an ideal community 'within' their real social situation" (1996, 322).[6] As idealizations, both communities are abstractions from concrete experience. Indeed, Habermas's purely linguistic discourse not only abstracts from non- and prelinguistic forms of communication, but also translates speech acts into "specialized codes" and "organized relationships" (1996, 437). He justifies these multiple—and parallel—moves by maintaining that

> the know-how informing argumentative practices represents a point of convergence where participants, however diverse their backgrounds, can at least intuitively meet in their efforts to reach an understanding. In all languages and in every language community, such concepts as truth, rationality, justification, and consensus, even if interpreted differently and applied according to different criteria, play *the same grammatical role.* (1996, 311)

Regarding cultural differences in communication styles, Habermas replies, "Even if one grants this, however, the worst one should expect is that the *explication* of our antecedently acquired practical knowledge will exhibit perspectival distortions" (1996, 311).

Together Habermas's successive arguments on behalf of ideal speech, communicative rationality, and legal constitutionalism raise the question: Why construe democratic discourse primarily in terms of a universal rationality to the detriment of its rhetorical contexts? What and, more important, who is lost when we abstract from non- and prelinguistic communication and translate linguistic forms into a partially delinguistified and highly institutionalized legal discourse?

Mixed Metaphors: From Voice to Text

> Writing and print isolate. There is no collective noun or concept for readers corresponding to "audience." (Walter Ong, *Orality and Literacy: The Technologizing of the Word* 1991, 74)

In his narrative of "linguistification," Habermas has focused on the transition from sacred to secular society, a process he understands as "rationalization." More recently, in the wake of the 9/11 terrorist attacks, he tempered this "methodological atheism," including his claim that secular communities tend to either replace or exploit religious faith (Mendietta 2002, 23). Habermas now gives renewed attention to the "existential relevance" of religion and the possibility that secular society can coexist with reasonable, that is, reflective, religious faiths. He also acknowledges that the boundaries between religious and secular validity claims are often fluid and porous (2003, 108–109). In chapter five, I reconsider this relationship between religious and political convictions in the context of civil rights music. Here my focus is another important transition obscured by Habermas's narrative of linguistification as secularization: the shift from orality to literacy. As Habermas tells the story, linguistic communication is the product of literate and, hence, modern, societies. The non- and prelinguistic forms of communication from which he distinguishes his rational discourse are the oral features of speech acts. Yet Habermas gives the cultural biases of his textually based theory of communicative rationality scant attention.

To better understand these biases I revisit Walter Ong's well-known distinction between orality and literacy in greater detail. In oral cultures, verbal expression involves magical powers, embodied experience, and archaic unities. "Sound cannot be sounding without the use of power" and, as a moving force, it unifies worlds—interior and exterior, self and other, and animals and spirits (1991, 32, 72). Since sound occurs in space-time, words are actions or events, and meanings are context-dependent. Context includes "not, as in a dictionary, simply other words, but . . . also gestures, vocal inflections, facial expression, and the entire human, existential setting in which the real, spoken word always occurs" (1991, 47). Knowledge (or "intelligence") is correspondingly "aggregative" and "pragmatic," and remains close to the lifeworld. Human interactions are "agonistically-toned" ritual struggles between "good and evil, virtue and vice, villains and heroes." These interactions are also "empathetic and participatory"; individuals' (re)actions are "encased in the communal reaction, the communal 'soul.'" Oral societies are correspondingly "conservative," "repetitive," and "traditionalist" (1991, 42–46).

According to Ong, the technology of writing transformed oral into literate societies: "It [writing] initiated what print and computers only continue, the reduction of dynamic sound to quiescent space, the separation of the word from the living present, where alone spoken words can exist" (1991, 82). Writing introduces a "new sensory world," a world of visually presented verbal material. Letters and words represent sounds as commodities, objects, or things separate(d) from their contexts. According to Ong, "Writing and print isolate. There is no collective noun or concept for readers corresponding to 'audience'" (1991, 74). Whereas "the total merger of knower and known in a holistic, formulaic experience made virtually impossible any programmatic developments in abstract thought," writing "ma[kes] possible the separation of the knower and the known, the substitution of knowledge-by-analysis for knowledge-by-empathy" (1977, 20, 36). Not surprisingly, literate cultures tend to overvalue the "book-learned" and "book-learning," and to undervalue practical experience, spiritual inspiration, and traditional knowledge(s). With mass literacy, the devaluation of these experiential knowledges is generalized, internalized, and expressed in deference to the "experts." For this reason, Jack Goody characterizes the transition from orality to literacy as the "scholarization," not the secularization, of society (1993).

Habermas's theory of communicative rationality is historically and conceptually linked to the textually based speech of literate societies. According to Habermas, the public use of reason began in the reading rooms, salons, and coffeehouses of a literary public sphere. Here, critical publics and rational subjects developed in tandem: "They formed the public sphere of a rational-critical debate in the world of letters within which the subjectivity originating in the interiority of the conjugal family, by communicating with itself, attained clarity about itself" (1991d, 51). Universal rights protected private points of view (as well as private property), while simultaneously allowing for their wider public expression. As Habermas puts it: "These rules, because universally valid, secured a space for the individuated person; because they were objective, they secured a space for what was subjective; because they were abstract, for what was most concrete" (1991d, 54). Only individuals who possessed a degree of "inner freedom" and, hence, the capacity to resist political compulsions, were prepared to engage in democratic politics (Leet 2004).

The early bourgeois public formed as a "reading public," but one in which individuality was directed outward and was "audience-oriented." Habermas maintains that it was not only a "republic of scholars," but a public that was "in principle inclusive" (1991d, 37), open to all "who were adept at [the public use of reason]" (1991d, 105). In any case, it was "immersed within a more inclusive public of all private people, persons who—insofar as they were propertied and educated—as readers, listeners, and spectators could avail themselves via the market of the objects that were subject to discussion" (1991d, 37). While participating in available cultural developments—philosophy, literature, art, theater—individual citizens also honed their critical reason and common sense. Here Habermas initially finds the potential for building an oppositional (as distinct from an "official") public, a potential, which, he later argues, the reification of private life and the commodification of culture gradually erodes.

In modern democracies, "the echo of private experiences," best expressed in the "existential language(s)" of the "'literary' public sphere," continues to be heard, however faintly, in "the diverse voices of this public" (1996, 365). Extending the model of a "reading public," Habermas argues that democratic citizens continue to "put forward 'texts' that always reveal the same subtext, which refers to the critical function of the public sphere in general" (1996, 369). In this way, "subcultural" or "partial" publics remain "porous" and "nonexclusionary": "The one text of 'the' public sphere, a text continually extrapolated and extending radially in all directions, is divided by internal boundaries into arbitrarily small texts for which everything else is context; yet one can always build hermeneutical bridges from one text to the next" (1996, 374). However, even as he advocates this "diffusion" of public discourses, Habermas admits that it "in turn requires a background political culture that is egalitarian, divested of all educational privileges, and thoroughly intellectual" (1996, 490).

In her work on the French Revolution, Joan Landes claims that Habermas has not adequately explored how the model of a "reading public" shapes "the symbolic structure of bourgeois representation." Landes doubts that Habermas's "normative subject is sufficiently multidimensional, embodied, or gendered to account for the organization of power in different cultural settings" (1995, 108, 92). As we saw, Habermas's speech act theory defines competent performances in textually based terms, as providing reasons for claims. In an unusually revealing passage, Habermas relegates nonverbal aspects of speech acts to "infrastructure" and says that "A bodily movement is an element of an action but not an action"

(1984, 96). Landes argues that this Habermasian model of communication not only brackets inequalities of education and property that restrict access to public discourse, but also prescribes universal roles for citizen-speakers. To be admitted as part of public discourse, interests and opinions that are expressed must be general/izable. To be general, they must also be disembodied or, at least, linguistified. In other words, Habermas's ideal of symmetrical relationships can be attained only if bodily differences and emotional affects are excluded from communication processes. Landes concludes that Habermas's speakers-cum-readers are little more than "talking heads" (1995, 103). It is their disembodiment that allows them to "stand-in" for absent others, to represent them. This symbolic structure of bourgeois representation presumes "a body which was also a non-body," a superiority to physical existence which is arguably both male-ordered and class-based (Outram quoted in Landes, 1995, 103). Paralleling Ong's remarks about "learned languages," to disembody reason as Habermas does is simultaneously to engender it—middle-class male.

However, what such critiques fail to notice is that Habermas employs another metaphor—voice-is-music—that implicitly acknowledges the cultural limitations of his discourse ideal. Habermas's references to sound/ing and, more specifically, voice/s are as infrequent as they are significant. They disclose the more concrete, diverse, embodied experiences of injustice, oppression, and suffering, which find expression in civil society. For Habermas, "voice" is the register of subjective interiority and critical publicity. In *The Structural Transformation of the Public Sphere*, he says "the 'sense of the people,' 'the common voice,' and 'the general cry of the people,' and finally 'the public spirit' denoted from this time onward an entity to which the opposition could appeal. . . ." (1991d, 64). In more recent writings, Habermas claims that "in the diverse voices of this public, one hears the echo of private experiences that are caused throughout society by the externalities (and internal disturbances) of various functional systems—and even by the state apparatus on whose regulatory activities the complex and poorly coordinated subsystems depend" (1996, 365). He cautions "intellectuals in general" and, specifically, feminist "spokeswomen," to delay judgment until "all those affected have had an effective opportunity to voice their demands for rights on the basis of concrete experiences of violated integrity, discrimination, and oppression" (1996, 426). And, he criticizes policy that "suppresses the voices of those who alone could *say* what the currently relevant reasons are for equal or unequal treatment" (1996, 420). He writes of a "resonant political culture" (1996, 461), a "vibrant civil society" (1996, 471), and worries that eventually the public sphere may no longer form a "sounding board" for political systems (1996, 343). In a highly metaphorical passage, he states, "Civil society is composed of those more or less spontaneous emergent associations, organizations, and movements that, attuned to how societal problems resonate in the private life spheres, distill and transmit such reactions in amplified form to the public sphere" (1996, 367). Regarding the political system, he distinguishes "articles in a bill of rights," which "result from political upheavals or revolutions" and "resonate with a suffered injustice" from the "professionally formulated or developed law of legal scholars" (1996, 389).

The vocal metaphors at work here are doubly obscured, first, by restricting oral expression to spoken words and, next, by translating those words into public "texts." When other aspects of voice are acknowledged, for example, the embodied sounds and e/motions of crying, laughing, singing, yelling, etc., the gender assumptions that inform Habermas's discourse ideal become increasingly apparent.[7] In patriarchal cultures, voice arguably conjures up a fantasy of origins—both desired and feared. Infants recognize (m)others' sounds before their bodies, and mothers still play the primary role in early language acquisition, transforming the infant (the Latin *infans* means non-speaking) into a "user of words." The maternal voice has been described as a "blanket of sound," a "sonorous envelope," an "acoustic space [which is] the originary psychic space." Female vocality reinvokes a "primordial experience of corporeal harmony," a deeply desired fusion with maternal/musical sound (Silverman 1988, 72, 96). Since the mother/child union also threatens to engulf, female vocality must be confined and displaced. Women's voices may be cast as too emotional, too irrational, too material, too spiritual; they pose a potential threat to the civilized, rational/ized, symbolic order. According to Dunn and Jones, "the mastering of that threat is enacted . . . discursively, through the containment of her utterance within a textuality identified as masculine, thus opposing her literal, embodied vocality to his metaphorical, disembodied 'voice'" (1994, 7). Kaja Silverman describes how this female voice serves as an "acoustic mirror" for the male subject. "Whereas the mother's voice initially functions as the acoustic mirror in which the child discovers its identity and voice, it later functions as the acoustic mirror in which the male subject hears all the repudiated elements of his infantile babble" (1988, 81). Male subjectivity is based in simultaneous process of corporeal and psychic separation: the "music of life," so to speak, is lost. In a fascinating discussion of voice, Linda Goehr argues that "music" becomes "a repository" for everything a philosophical theory constrained by the authority of reason cannot capture (1998, 18–19). This extraordinary meaning of music partly explains its power for politics.

To return for now to Habermas, his mixed metaphors convey great ambivalence about the political presence of embodied voices even as they reveal the problems music poses for rational communication. It seems that musical sound—an affective, creative, material, spiritual power—that animates civil society must be confined there or, more precisely, translated into a public discourse defined by its exclusion. A "reading public" can adequately mediate between everyday life, ordinary speech and expert cultures, as well as between systems media and lifeworld contexts. When "voice/s" are channeled by rights and laws, and expressed in opinions and votes, they are ostensibly "cleansed" and "tamed." Yet Habermas's textual metaphors ultimately merely displace the problem of music. Although they preempt the cacophony of voice/s, they cannot resolve their dissonant sounds into political harmony.[8] As we have seen, speech-as-text acts presuppose an abstract and, for that reason, merely superficial, discursive consciousness; an "eviscerated" body politic is only skin deep.

With his musical metaphors Habermas discloses the deeper, subconscious, possibly unconscious, intuitions and impulses, which animate his theory of deliberative democracy. According to Young, the "body aesthetic" of Western reason tends to associate oppressed groups more closely with the body and, then, devalues embodied experience as less-than-rational (1990, 139). Although Habermas might wish otherwise, his communicative rationality is no exception: some cultures are less rational and more musical than others, but all citizens ideally translate their private voices into public texts. Habermas's civil society may "resonate" and "vibrate," but not with the sounds of its subcultures.[9] The public sphere he describes as "a 'wild' complex that resists organization as a whole" and an "anarchic structure" is "tamed" or, at least, caged, by its public text (1996, 307–308). It becomes and remains the "*always already familiar*" and, hence, comfortable, lifeworld of a "reading public."

One need not disparage Habermas's rhetoric as strategic to recognize that his metaphors reflect culturally-specific experiences and imperatives. To his credit, Habermas urges philosophers to avoid just such biases: "the philosopher ought to explain the moral point of view, and—as far as possible—justify the claim to universality of this explanation, showing why it does not merely reflect the moral intuitions of the average, male, middle-class member of a modern Western society. Anything further than that is a matter for moral discourse between participants" (1986, 160). In this respect, Habermas's theory of communicative rationality is "ideology and simultaneously more than ideology" (Dryzek 2000, 88). He maintains that cultural traditions, including natural languages and aesthetic styles, always serve a dual purpose. They are both the "stencils" by which "needs are shaped," and the "medium" in which "needs can seek and find alternative interpretations" (Habermas 1979a, 93). Rather than ascribe needs to individuals, Habermas allows for their continuing interpretation through discourse—as long as the needs are, in principle, "generalizable." Yet, "generalizability" is the seemingly insoluble problem. Although individuals can articulate alternative interpretations of their needs, they cannot challenge their prescribed interpretive roles. Here, the circle closes: by definition competent speakers follow universal procedures based on particular, that is, middle-class male, experiences. These procedures, in turn, force individuals with different communication styles to develop the "double consciousness" typical of culturally imperialized groups. They must not only split their public roles from their private selves, a split modern, Western society expresses in various dualisms, such as, mind/body, reason/emotion, and culture/nature. They are also positioned as an/Other within the dominant discourse, that is, as body to mind, emotion to reason, nature to culture. As I explore later, the musical practices of social movements often attempt to resist, subvert, and/or transcend these binaries.

For Habermas, the promise of modern democracy rests elsewhere, in large part, on the "linguistification of the sacred," a process of rationalization that opens up the possibility of secular governmental authority. Habermas fears the potential regression of modern societies to the unmediated experience of premodern world views, and he regards projects to recover cultural traditions, to re-create authentic communities, as too integrative, too unreflective. Sociopolitical interactions, he claims, must continually recognize the vulnerability of individuals and guarantee the inviolability of rights. According to Habermas, "autonomous and publically conducted debate" is the best intersubjective complement to "the responsible assumption of one's life history" (1990, 261–262). When properly extended to legal institutions, "the realization of basic rights is a process *that secures the private autonomy of equally entitled citizens only in step with the activation of their political autonomy*" (1996, 426). Only the discourse of law enables nonviolent solidarity between the permanent strangers of modern societies (Dean 1996). Legal norms guarantee equal respect and shared recognition and, when the legal rights are effectively protected, they mediate between universal principles and lifeworld values. For these reasons, Habermas maintains that "the discourse principle is intended to assume the shape of a principle of democracy only by way of legal institutions" (1996, 121).

Habermas admits that communicative rationality may reproduce forms of internal violence (what Lee calls "symbolic domination"), but he insists that at these crucial junctures it remains open to criticism. His discourse theory does not defend "intellectualization" or deny "latent instinctual conflicts" (1991b, 180). Instead, he regards "unconsciously motivated actions . . . as a latent reversal of the differentiation between strategic and communicative action, a dedifferentiation that is hidden from the actor and others." Such "intrapsychic disturbances of communication" may permit a subject to "deceive himself about the fact that he is objectively violating the shared presuppositions of action oriented toward reaching understanding" (1991b, 188). The problem is that Habermas's mixed—textual and vocal—metaphors, suggest he may also be so deceived. At Young's level of ontological integrity or basic security, his rational discourse leaves few openings for symbolic resistance. Habermas presents communicative rationality as a selective recovery of what he deems "progressive" lifeworld values. However, my concern is that *his* were never left behind.

The regression to "savagery" Habermas fears may threaten democratic equality less than his—and other democratic theorists'—denial of affective and corporeal politics does (Tambornino 2000). Indeed, Habermas may deliver democratic citizens to the very political dangers he fears. His refusal to cultivate aesthetic sensibilities, including aesthetic individuality and even aesthetic reason, limits his capacity to resist the tendency of Western reason to commodify, objectify, and subjugate an/Other (Coles 1997; Leet 2004; Morris 2001; Schoolman 2001). Although Habermas's musical metaphors disclose the promise of consciously reembodied, more inclusive, and more radical, forms of discourse, their world-disclosive potential is not fully realized in his or other theories of deliberative democracy (Dryzek 2000; Young 2000). I conclude this chapter with some preliminary thoughts about the role music might play in democratic communication.

Voice, Music, and Democracy

> Nothing will change without the intervening, effective, innovative energy of social movements, and without the utopian images and energies that motivate such movements. (Habermas, "A Conversation About Questions of Political Theory" 1997, 133–134)

Habermas's metaphors reveal the larger rhetorical context that informs his theory of communicative rationality. They also disclose another layer of culture, register of discourse, and level of experience: voice as music. His vocal metaphors implicitly acknowledge the moving sounds of speech and the embodied voices of speakers. They invoke the diverse experiences of democratic citizens, and they convey differences that can—often with considerable risk—be publicly voiced, but are not easily translated into the terms of public discourse. Earlier, I described the abstract symmetries of idealized speech as a culturally-specific, textually-based, body aesthetic or, more precisely, a disembodied aesthetic. Recently, musicologists have begun to call for an aesthetic that can convey "how music works and undoes us when we stop observing and enter it." Quoting Barthes, Barbara Engh describes how this aesthetic differs from formal music theory: "Let the first semiology manage, if it can, with the system of notes, scales, tones, chords, and rhythms; what we want to perceive and follow is the effervescence of the beats . . . a second semiology, that of the body in a state of music" (1993, 73–74). Earlier, I suggested that the aesthetic value at work here is, what Harrell calls, "profundity." The experience of profundity recognizes "an intrinsic value in the biological fact of life established previsually, therefore probably prenatally" (Harrell 1992, 20–21). The music of our bodies—their gestures, movements, rhythms, and tones—reminds us of our common human being (McNeill 1995). Although profundity taps into visceral responses, it seems important to reiterate that it is not for this reason "primitive." Harrell finds examples of profundity in the artistic creations, especially the music, of all cultures (1992, 68–70, 91). Ellen Koskoff's comprehensive definition of music describes the body/brain/culture linkage here. Music is

> "raw" sound (i.e., natural/supernatural sound) turned into human sound (i.e., efficacious, beautiful, formed, useful sound) through the process of using a music-culture (a shared ideational system, prescribing a performer, performance context, use, style, etc.). (1991, 775)

As an experience of shared humanity, music is also unavoidably and fundamentally political. Contra theories of autonomous music, Lydia Goehr writes: "Music is political already in virtue of the fact that music is a practice of human expression or performance working itself out in the world, in particular communities, through the medium of melody" (1998, 128).

Habermas occasionally recognizes that art, including music, "enters into a language game that is no longer that of aesthetic criticism but belongs rather to everyday communicative practices" (1985c, 414). These seemingly ordinary aesthetic experiences, he argues, actually have extraordinary validity: they possess a "singularly illuminating power to open our eyes to what is seemingly familiar, to disclose anew an apparently familiar reality. They transform established relations between self and world" (1985c, 415). Yet, when Habermas searches for lifeworld resources to counter the "siege" of systems media, when he would open up the "sluices" between lifeworld and system, he finds only the textually-based public discourse of legal rights. No wonder he laments the demise of citizens-cum-readers and fears the images and sounds of more penetrating mass media, like cinema, music, and, especially, television. Of the latter, he writes: "They draw the eyes and ears of the public under their spell but at the same time, by taking away its distance, place it under their 'tutelage'" (1991d, 171). Aesthetic experience, he suggests, all too easily loses its critical perspective and becomes an object of consumer culture. The unfortunate result is that widespread apathy and conformity overshadow potential sources of political opposition, including progressive social movements, in modern democratic societies.

And yet it was Habermas who claimed that the critiques of mass culture mounted by first-generation critical theorists were too monolithic, too pessimistic. Whereas they exaggerated the dangers of instrumental reason, I want to suggest that Habermas's fears of an aestheticized politics are similarly exaggerated, and the other side of the same dialectical coin of Enlightenment "reason." I have already shown that music—the musicality of speech—can be dimly heard behind/beneath/beyond the rational communication of Habermas's deliberative democracy. Yet there is something profoundly unsatisfying in relegating music to this limited role, in excluding it from public and, more specifically, political, life. A remark of Ernest Bloch regarding post-Kantian German philosophers seems apt here: they tend to "use music as a springboard to launch *their* theories, *their* philosophies, *their universal panaceas* into the world, and forget that its true purpose is simply to be moving" (quoted in Goehr 1998, 46).

With his musical metaphors, Habermas invokes embodied voices and gestures toward music as a form of public discourse, even as he enshrines the cultural biases of (his) communicative rationality. Ironically, it is his *metaphors* that disclose the possibility of a more inclusive, more radical, democratic discourse, one animated and energized by musical experience. How, we might ask, does movement music—blues, folk, gospel, jazz, rap, rock—actually work to "transform the totality"? Music of the feminist and civil rights movements, music that has changed—or moved—the shape of democratic politics is the subject of later chapters. Although the dangers of political aestheticism persist here, I hope to have at least shown that Habermas's "rational/ized" public discourse does not—and cannot—entirely avoid them. To further develop that aspect of my argument, I first explore the musical form designed to bring the diverse voices of civil society into democratic harmony: the symphony orchestra.

CHAPTER THREE

Rawlsian Harmonies: Orchestrating Consensus

. . . the notion of society as a social union of social unions shows how it is possible for a regime of liberty not only to accommodate a plurality of conceptions of the good but also to coordinate the various activities made possible by human diversity into a more comprehensive good to which everyone can contribute and in which each can participate. (John Rawls, *Political Liberalism* 1996, 323)

We have a male harpist, and two ladies. If you ask how noticeable the gender is with these colleagues, my personal experience is that this instrument is so far at the edge of the orchestra that it doesn't disturb our emotional unity, the unity I would strongly feel, for example, when the orchestra starts really cooking with a Mahler symphony. Then, I sense very strongly and simply that only men sit around me. And . . . I would not want to gamble with this unity. (Helmut Zehetner, first violin, Vienna Philharmonic, quoted by Osborne 1999, 7)

I used to think about guns and robbing people. Now I feel like I'm progressing. (Lenna, National System of Children's Orchestras, Venezuela, quoted by Jones 1999, 8)

The rhetoric of John Rawls's theory of justice provides an excellent illustration of the cultural underpinnings of deliberative democrats' discourse ideal.[1] Like Habermas, Rawls relies heavily on intuitive ideas that constitute a liberal political culture, specifically, on society as a fair system of cooperation composed of reasonable individuals who possess a sense of justice and a concept of the good. These shared cultural intuitions allow Rawls to distinguish his later political liberalism, the product of an overlapping consensus on principles of justice, from earlier more comprehensive liberal doctrines, including his own (Dombrowski 2001, 84). However, Rawls's distinction between a political and a metaphysical liberalism remains clearer to him than to his most sympathetic critics. The problem is not only the obvious continuity between Rawls's works, including the fact that "the phrase 'justice as fairness' (as well as the original position, the veil of ignorance, the priority of the right to the good, and the two principles of justice) is retained in the later Rawls under the umbrella term *political liberalism. . . .*" (Dombrowski 2001, viii). It is also that, as Dombrowski notes, "Rawls himself correctly speaks of a 'unity' of both 'spirit and content' to TJ and PL" (2001, x). To his critics, Rawls's liberalism seems to presume the very principles of justice that he claims representative individuals produce in their overlapping consensus. No wonder numerous scholars claim that Rawls's theory exhibits "circularity," "displace[s] the vital voices and self-determination of the citizenry," and creates a "too expansive" concept of the reasonable (Odedoyin 2000, 341; Schleffler 1994, 20; Wenar 1995, 39). As one critic puts the problem: "Though Rawls does not describe in detail how the intuitive ideas tie in with the choice of principles in the original position, it is clear that the intuitive ideas are represented by central features of the original position and the deliberations of the representative individuals" (Klosko 1997, 636).

In this chapter, I suggest that Rawls does describe how cultural intuitions motivate his principles of justice, but he does so in a way philosophers might least expect. His political liberalism gives philosophers the reasonable arguments for principles of justice among free, equal citizens of a democratic society that they seek. However, Rawls does not limit himself to the tools of reason. He also employs metaphors to reveal the intuitive ideals that animate his liberal political culture and, with it, the deep structure of his theory of justice. Rawls draws his concept of a well-ordered society—a "social union of social unions"—from Wilhelm von Humboldt, a fascinating, but seldom-noticed, source.[2] Paralleling von Humboldt's use of musical metaphors, Rawls characterizes liberal democracy as a symphony orchestra. I explore the cultural and political implications of Rawls's "symphonic justice" at some length. The metaphor situates Rawls's overlapping consensus in historical context and, I argue, reveals the cultural limitations of the political project that undergirds his theory of justice.

Hearing the Music

> Rawls is pulled by the demand that things be still at bottom. (Connolly, *Why I Am Not a Secularist* 1999, 69)

Rawls's metaphors in *A Theory of Justice* and *Political Liberalism* reveal his efforts to control the power of embodied voices in democratic discourse. Like other deliberative democrats, he repeatedly distinguishes reason from rhetoric and expresses his distrust for the latter. At best, he denigrates rhetoric as mere style. He writes: "Now all ways of reasoning—whether individual, associational, or political—must acknowledge certain common elements: the concept of judgment, principles of inference, and rules of evidence, and much else, otherwise they would not be ways of reasoning but perhaps rhetoric or means of persuasion" (1996, 220). He then adds: "We are concerned with reason, not simply with discourse" (1996, 220). Rhetoric enters into Rawls's understanding of discourse only indirectly, as the cultural context within which speech acts acquire their shared meanings. Rawls understands cultural traditions, including the proper use of language, as "rule-based" practices (1955, 37). He claims that actions, including speech acts, can only be meaningfully performed in the "stage-setting"—or context—of the rules that prescribe their practice. When actions occur out-of-context, they will "fail to count as a form of action which the practice specifies" (1955, 37). They will be understood, more precisely, misunderstood, as something other than what they are (1955, 37). To illustrate this point, Rawls draws an analogy to baseball: he notes that anyone "can throw a ball, run, or swing a peculiarly shaped piece of wood . . . ," but "striking out, stealing a base, balking, etc. are all actions which can only happen in a game. . . ." (1955, 37). He concludes that "the practice is logically prior to particular cases: unless there is the practice the terms referring to actions specified by it lack a sense" (1955, 37). The logical priority of practices limits their critical scrutiny and prompts Rawls to include the following disclaimer with his description of "reason":

> What we affirm is a tradition that incorporates ideals and virtues which meet the tests of our reason and which answer to our deepest desires and affections. Of course, many persons may not examine their acquired beliefs and ends but take them on faith, or be satisfied that they are matters of custom and tradition. They are not to be criticized for this, for in the liberal view there is no political or social evaluation of conceptions of the good within the limits permitted by justice. (1996, 314)

From within these liberal practices, Rawls distinguishes "the [sic] idea of reasoning and judgment [which] applies to our moral and political statements" from "simply . . . voicing our psychological state" (1996, 110–111). Elaborating on the distinction, he employs "voice" to describe "subversive advocacy": "If free political speech is guaranteed . . . serious grievances do not go unrecognized or suddenly become highly dangerous. They are publicly voiced; and in a moderately well-governed regime they are at least to some degree taken into account" (1996, 347). However, ". . . revolutionaries don't simply shout: 'Revolt! Revolt!' They give reasons" (1996, 346). Rawls associates "voice" with expressions of injustice and suffering, which become politically effective only after translation into the terms of public reason.

Rawls's vocal metaphors have received little scholarly attention, even though they are repeatedly echoed in commentaries on his work. For example, William Connolly claims Rawls's "rendering of the separation between the private and the public makes it tone-deaf to multiple modes of suffering and subordination currently subsisting below the public register of justice" (1999, 10). Connolly's recent work on "neuropolitics" or "the politics through which cultural life mixes into the composition of body/brain processes" further develops his critique of the excessive "intellectualism" of Rawls and Habermas. He proposes "a perspective that appreciates the dense interweaving of genetic endowment, image, movement, sound, rhythm, smell, touch, technique, trauma, exercise, thinking, and sensibility" (Connolly 2002, 12.3). These "corporeal/spiritual contexts," Connolly argues, cannot be reduced to "disembodied tokens of representation" (2002, 40.9). Nor are they adequately represented by essentialized or naturalized biological aspects of human being. For Connolly, people experience difference as a layered complex of relays and relations between conscious and visceral experiences. "Dispositional memories," "side-perceptions," and "proto-thoughts" accompany the highly disciplined processes of rational thinking, and sometimes even supercede them (Connolly 2002). By ruling these processes "out of politics" except as they are translated into the terms of public reason, Rawls asks citizens to be "silent" where conversation is most needed, where conflicts are likely to be most intense (Connolly 1999, 64, 68). He precludes exploration of the experiences—whether mystical, subliminal, or both—that "animate" and "energize" our politics. For Connolly, "to think is to move something," a reference to which I return when discussing the politics of "movement music" (2002, 104). A public reason that suppresses or excludes the visceral register prevents citizens from "moving" themselves and others toward an ethos of generosity (Connolly 1999, 68).

Contra Rawls's "fixed moral code" and "abstract conception of the person," Connolly embraces "justice as an essentially ambiguous practice, insufficient to itself," but oriented toward "the plurovocity of being" (1999, 10–11, 62–70). Instead of Rawls's "drive to stillness," which "freezes" politics at the level of justice, Connolly proposes increased "attunement" to the "persistence of becoming" (1999, 70).

Susan Bickford (1996) also employs vocal, more specifically, musical, metaphors to discuss Rawlsian liberalism. She claims that Rawls's desire for an overlapping consensus on principles of justice denies the "dissonance of democracy." Like Connolly, Bickford asks what motivates Rawls's distinction between a metaphysical liberalism and his own more political version. The original position, she claims, "even if not a 'metaphysical doctrine about the nature of the self,' surely must reflect something important about the kinds of social and political creatures we are" (1996, 8). Bickford argues that Rawls builds public identity around "what enables us to agree," a shared capacity to reason, but one that is defined from within his culturally specific and, hence, less than fully representative, position. "The result (however unintended) of these constraints on public identity is not merely that citizens do not argue about the good in the political realm, but that they do not argue at all" (1996, 9). For Bickford, Rawls's theory of justice "evokes an image of citizens as traffic on a highway, and politics as a kind of traffic control that steers us away from interfering with each other's journey" (1996, 10). Where Connolly hears a deafening stillness, Bickford sees orderly movement. They agree, however, that Rawls imposes an overlapping consensus on the very citizens he would protect from comprehensive doctrines, including his own. Even a pluralistic liberalism, they suggest, has its own fundamental convictions.

Unlike Connolly and Bickford, who offer only metaphorical glosses on Rawls's theory, George Armstrong Kelly analyzes a Rawlsian metaphor—the "veil of ignorance"—in depth. He explores its connections with language and, by association, voice. According to Kelly, Rawls is "a formidably cultured writer" who writes "a sort of congealed history," the prescriptions of which are "contingent upon common understandings" (1996, 360–361). Rawls's "veil of ignorance," he argues, is drawn from "the culture of Hellenic and Hebraic classics, seen through the Enlightenment and through German idealism, through Victorian literature, English political economy, and their legacies" (1996, 364). Kelly writes:

> The veil of ignorance is also a "veil of language"—fixed in such a way that social members can communicate "in an ideal speech situation" (to use Habermas's phrase) before becoming exposed to the language of the tribe, weaving the one language into the others as if through a Humboldtian "delicate veil" or a Tennysonian "lucid veil"; a tegument so close to the mind's eye that it is hardly perceived in the passage into the world of social appearances. (1996, 364)

As Kelly presents it, Rawls's veil of ignorance guards his noumenal realm with its principles of justice and precedes discursive engagement with the phenomenal world. Like Tennyson, Rawls separates his idealist theory of language from an empiricist one, and penetrates the barrier between them only "by veiled means—the power of memory contrived in language" (1996, 348). Like von Humboldt, Rawls creates a sense of warmth as the veil is gradually lifted, a diffused "light made twilight," rather than the harsh rays of abstract reason (Kelly 1996, 348).

Although Rawls does not explicitly credit von Humboldt with his veil metaphor, the philosophical connection proves helpful for understanding the cultural underpinnings of his theory of justice. Von Humboldt, who regards metaphors as representing the *Gestalt* of a people, expresses his synthesis of enlightened reason and romantic sentiments through aesthetic and organic analogies. Among the arts, he regards music as the best expression of human energies, since it combines a "sequence of time" with "a theme, to which we can supply an endless number of texts," and allows the listener to respond "free[ly] and naturally from his own resources" (1969, 72–73). Of various types of music, "the human voice, of equal melodiousness and quality, . . . more than a lifeless instrument" stimulates a harmony of sensual and spiritual impressions (1969, 74). Von Humboldt writes, "The aesthetic feeling, in virtue of which the sensuous is to us a veil of the spiritual, and the spiritual the living principle of the world of sense, is everywhere unmistakable" (1969, 75). He contrasts this deep equilibrium of body and spirit, itself a source of moral reform, with the cold reason of analytic philosophy.

Rawls refers to von Humboldt twice, once in *A Theory of Justice* and again in *Political Liberalism*, each time to credit him with the concept of a "social union of social unions" (1999a, 459–460; 1996, 320). In *A Theory of Justice*, Rawls discusses at some length how social union differs from other concepts of social cooperation: "it is important not to confuse the idea of social union with the high value put upon human diversity and individuality [romanticism]; . . . or with the conception of the good as the harmonious fulfillment of natural powers by (complete) individuals [socialism]; nor, finally with gifted individuals, artists, and statesmen, and so on achieving this for the rest of mankind [utilitarianism]" (1999a, 460n4 [inserts mine]). According to Rawls, a social union is defined as a community of individuals who have developed and coordinated their different and complementary powers. Only von Humboldt (and possibly Adam Smith) have successfully depicted this sense of unity. Rawls describes its ethos: "persons need one another since it is only in active cooperation with others that any one's talents can be realized, and then in large part by the efforts of all. Only in the activities of social union can the individual be complete" (1996, 321). For Rawls the possibility of social union is contingent upon the presence of basic liberties; social cooperation and self-respect work in tandem to promote a "*sense* of justice." Through social union citizens become participants in a larger good that spans generations, and simultaneously helps sustain their pursuit of individual life-plans.

By crediting von Humboldt for his concept of social

union, Rawls acknowledges the challenge of organizing, what Connolly calls, "the affective element of intersubjectivity" (2002, 104). Rawls's concept of social union responds to questions about what "moves the parties in the original position" to adopt principles of justice, and how "to help fashion" the necessary "political will" when it is lacking (1996, 297, 307). Rawls's original position might be seen as a representative example of social union. It places citizens behind a "veil of ignorance" to model fair terms of social cooperation: impartiality, reciprocity, symmetry, and universality. In the absence of knowledge about their social status, citizens are encouraged to reflect and clarify the meaning of social cooperation (1996, 26). Their agreement on principles of justice provides a second, more complex, example of social union. In *A Theory of Justice,* Rawls describes overlapping consensus as a shared conclusion derived from different premises, or the area where different conceptions of justice overlap (1999a, 340). Later, in *Political Liberalism,* overlapping consensus becomes a "freestanding political conception" that citizens can defend without threatening deeper religious and/or philosophical convictions (1996, 389). Although Rawls claims that the latter rests on a shared "basis of reasons," rather than a shared "*sense* of justice," his continuous reliance on von Humboldt and musical metaphors strongly suggests otherwise. Rawls's overlapping consensus, I argue, continues to rely on shared liberal intuitions. It emerges from "the fundamental idea of society as a fair system of cooperation and its companion ideas," rather than a "balance of forces" or "modus vivendi" among competing comprehensive doctrines (1996, 40). After citizens have agreed on principles of justice, they bring their comprehensive doctrines into politics only by translating them into the terms of public reason.

Rawls identifies many human activities amenable to the formation of social unions, with games as the most accessible and, for that reason, most democratic, example.[3] Games, like baseball, also clearly illustrate that social union is a rule-based practice with a structure of cooperation and/or competition that defines fair play. Game-theoretic assumptions about human beings as rational egoists fail adequately to characterize liberal society as a social union, however. In an important passage, Rawls uses a musical example to illustrate the moral limitations of game theory, including how it diverges from rule-based practices of justice.[4] Two musicians and housemates, Matthew (a trumpeter) and Luke (a pianist) seek a fair division of playing time. A connection exists between their preferences and their instruments: Matthew (with his obvious threat advantage) prefers both playing at once to neither playing and Luke would choose silence over cacophony. If they change instruments, then the power differential is simply reversed. Rawls considers another possibility, changing the music; he makes Matthew a jazz drummer and Luke a violinist who plays sonatas. On this analysis, he surmises, "it will be fair . . . for Matthew to play whenever and as often as he likes, assuming as it is plausible that he does not care whether Luke plays or not. Clearly something has gone wrong" (1999a, 116n10). By changing the music, Rawls illustrates what is missing in this musical game. Regardless of the allocation of playing time, Luke and Matthew lack "a suitable definition of a status quo that is acceptable from a moral point of view" (1999a, 116n10).[5]

We have already seen Rawls's attempts to designate such a status quo: the original position and the overlapping consensus on the principles of justice it supports. We have also seen his critics' claims that his theory of justice is, at best, circular and, at worst, impoverished in its reliance on material/spiritual intuitions it fails to include or sustain. I now turn to the metaphor Rawls chooses to reveal the deep structure of his theory of justice. When Rawls lifts the veil of ignorance, he reveals a well-ordered society, a social union of social unions, whose citizens are musicians, players in a symphony orchestra.

Overlapping Consensus as Symphony Orchestra

> A conductor once told his orchestra: "One eye has to be on the music, the other on the conductor; one ear is for listening to the

> orchestra, the other for one's own performance." (Shore, *Orchestra Speaks* 1938, 17)

Rawls uses his orchestral metaphor in both *A Theory of Justice* and *Political Liberalism,* including two versions of it in each work.[6] The two versions roughly parallel the original position behind the veil of ignorance and the liberal society that results from the principles of justice. In the first version, Rawls describes "a group of gifted musicians, all of whom have the same natural talents and who could, therefore, have learned to play equally well every instrument in the orchestra" (Rawls 1996, 321). Recognizing the impossibility of learning every instrument, let alone playing all of them simultaneously, each musician becomes proficient on a single instrument. "Thus, in this special case in which everyone's natural talents are identical, the group achieves, by a coordination of activities among peers, the same totality of capacities latent in each" (Rawls 1996, 321). Rawls's second version involves individuals who know that their musical gifts are unequal and different. They are nonetheless able to achieve a similar result, since their talents are complementary and they coordinate them properly.

Rawls's two renditions of "symphonic justice" correspond in interesting ways with the historical development of the European orchestra. The term "orchestra" derives from Greek theater, and first referred to the semicircular space at the front of the stage where the chorus sang and, only much later, where instrumental musicians played.[7] Early orchestras served their towns or villages as players and criers, performing at public ceremonies and church services, and sounding a warning when fires broke out and strangers approached. Their musicians were versatile and, since instruments were scarce, played whatever was available. The first orchestral compositions merely doubled singing voices, but gradually instrumental music began to replace voice parts. By the Renaissance, the doctrine of the affects associated different instruments with specific e/motions and attributed rhetorical qualities to orchestral works. Most music was "polyphonic," that is, it consisted of independent musical parts with roughly equal standing. Families of instruments ostensibly engaged in polyphonic conversations; strings "ruled" because they best imitated the emotional variation of the human voice (Bekker 1936).[8] Later, with the development of homophonic music, a clear distinction emerged between a melodic line and its chordal accompaniments. As a result, orchestral compositions changed "from the weaving of independent parts to a single dominating melody, supported by a steady progression of vertical harmonies"—and the symphony became possible (Rosen 1997, 29).

"Symphony" derives from the Greek "sym" meaning "together, similarly, alike" and "phone" for "sounding"; to "symphonize" is "to sing or sound together, in concert, or in harmony." More general connotations include "agreement, accord, concord, and congruity."[9] An orchestral version of the classical sonata, symphonic form follows a "discursive logic" and is often described as the musical "*Bildungsroman*" (Rothstein 1986, 539). Written in three or, sometimes, four movements, the symphony moves from harmonic stability (exposition) through instability (development) and then returns to stability (recapitulation).

Although this overall harmonic structure predominates in sonatas and symphonies, it is articulated through a series of individual melodies.[10] Eduard Rothstein characterizes the delicate balance of melody and harmony this requires: "Melody is feeling, harmony is law; melody provides expanse, harmony defines limits; melody can be considered an image of the self, harmony an image of society; melody is desire, harmony is order" (1986, 543).

Obvious parallels exist between the symphony orchestra and the liberal democratic ideals associated with European nation-building. For the music historian Paul Bekker, symphonic form mirrors the "unification of all individualities into a free community" (1936, 117). Numerous scholars of nineteenth-century music, philosophy, and politics agree. According to Lydia Goehr, classical style and, more specifically, symphonic form allows subjective freedom to express itself "within and against objective constraints" (1998, 1). Rosen summarizes the result: "In music, the classical style attacked the horizontal independence of the voices and the vertical independence of the harmony by isolating the phrase and articulating the structure" (1997, 29). He adds, "the simplest way to summarize classical form is as the symmetrical resolution of opposing forces" (Rosen 1997, 83). According to Marc Redfield, the association of aesthetic enculturation—or *Bildung*—with political development is a prerequisite for nation-building. Aesthetics, technics, politics, are inextricably linked, even when autonomous art, especially, music, is constructed as an/Other to reason. Redfield writes: "Civil society depends on the fundamental, perceptual, communication, and referential harmony, the *sensus communis,* to which aesthetic judgment testifies and that it works to produce. Training us for life in the nation-state, aesthetic education presupposes its own accomplishments as the foundation of the social itself" (2003, 16). Through music the nation-state could deepen the aesthetic experience of its citizen-subjects and create a nation of individuals capable of sensing ethical imperatives together. The symphony, with its carefully composed developmental logic and harmonic structure, mirrored the dangers posed by dissonant voices and resolved them into social consensus.

Rawls's orchestral metaphor evokes this liberal democratic resolution of the individual and society. Behind the veil of ignorance, individuals "forget" their position in society and their comprehensive doctrines; they could play any and all instruments. They orchestrate their combined interactions according to their cultural traditions and political intuitions (justice as fairness). The resulting symphony recognizes natural talents (moral capacities) and the complementary needs of individuals (primary goods). As Rawls's representative citizens make music together, their different melodies (reasonable comprehensive doctrines) assume and affirm a harmonic structure (reasonable overlapping consensus). Presumably, these citizens gradually become more proficient musicians and their sense of justice expands and deepens. When the veil—now a curtain—lifts, their performance mirrors three-part or four-part (including the original position) symphonic development. In successive movements, liberal-democratic citizens apply their principles of justice to constitutional, legislative, and judicial contexts. Although these applications require various modifications, the musicians make every effort to remain faithful to the "rule-based practice" that constitutes symphonic form.

One wonders, though, how Rawls's veiled musicians know the orchestral score, how they learn their musical parts. Regarding language-use behind the veil of ignorance, Michael Weiss argues, "As with the person who loses the context of the world in which he lives through suffering amnesia, when a person lives without a sense of self he does not merely make statements about society that are generic; he loses the ability to make fully meaningful statements" (1993, 538). Here Rawls's orchestral metaphor conveys a double meaning. It associates the original position with dim, early, memories of language. Like Habermas, Rawls invokes "profundity," the preverbal experience of rhythm and tone rooted in a "rudimentary recall . . . recognition of an intrinsic value in the biological fact of life established previsually, therefore probably prenatally" (Harrell 1992, 20–22). The orderly harmonies of classical form, as much as the driving rhythms of rock music, invoke a shared sense of bodily being (Harrell 1992, 68–70, 91). Behind the veil of ignorance, this literal *sense* of justice motivates Rawls's orchestral musicians to perform their "songs without words" (Bekker 1936, 37).[11] An alternative to noise or silence, their instrumental music reveals primal aspects of human experience that cannot be translated into the language of reason (Goehr 1998, 25–28).

Yet—and here is the second meaning—embodied voices also pose a potential threat to public reason. The "unisonance" of the nation, an imaginary community born out of distinct individuals, is disrupted by embodied sounds (Redfield 2003, 56). As we see later, some bodies, those racialized and sexualized as "different" or "other," are more disruptive to political unity than others. Rawls limits the disruptive power of these bodily differences by making his citizens instrumental musicians. As I discuss in chapter five, when instruments are played with body and soul, their sounds approximate human voice/s (Goehr 1998, 121). Jazz musicians who "make a horn speak" create improvised conversations among their personnified instruments. However, Rawls's citizens play detached or, at least, detachable instruments. As participants in overlapping consensus, each performs on a "voice prosthesis" and masters its part in the orchestral score (Silverman 1988). Rawls emphasizes rule-based compositional practices, rather than the musicians' bodies that animate and energize them. According to Goehr, "In musical or aesthetic terms, rules exist to be bent, broken, or ultimately left behind" (1998, 40). She continues, "A practice is closed when what could be a progressive ideal—and the formalist claim can be such—is used regressively to make rules and conditions sufficient in either ontological or explanatory terms" (1998, 41). With his combined emphases on instrumental music, formal structure, and harmonic order, Rawls portrays a symphony orchestra—and overlapping consensus—that is oddly unmusical.

Metaphysics as Metaphor

> Not an Emperor, and not a King, but stand there like one and conduct. (Wagner, quoted by Osborne 1999, 92)

In an unusual passage, Rawls acknowledges the transfer of meaning involved in metaphors: ". . . the name 'justice as fairness' . . . does not mean that the concepts of justice and fairness are the same, any more than the phrase 'poetry as metaphor' means that the concepts of poetry and metaphor are the same" (1999a, 11). Rawls has repeatedly stressed that justice and fairness share a concept of reciprocity, a virtue applicable only to rule-based or institutionalized practices. Of reciprocity, he writes: "A practice will strike the parties as conforming to the notion of reciprocity if none feels that, by participating in it, he or any of the others are taken advantage of or forced to give into claims which they do not accept as legitimate" (1971, 208). However, as we have seen, fair play involves more than following the rules of the game; it also requires sensing—feeling and perceiving—other citizens as fellow human beings. In other words, symphony or harmony requires more than the symmetrical structure modeled in the original position. To reinvoke Connolly, Rawls's theory is not still at bottom; there is e/motion beneath the ice. He taps into a deeper source of democratic sentiments, a "*sense* of justice" born from experiences of "profundity."

Rawls reveals this underlying foundation of his principles of justice with his orchestral metaphors.[12] They, in turn, reveal the European cultural and political origins of his liberalism. According to William Osborne, "The symphony orchestra is culturally isomorphic with the values of the European societies in which it developed" (1999, 71). We have already examined one such isomorphism: the harmonic resolution of individual and society central to liberal democratic nation-building. Osborne discusses this phenomenon in relation to two additional, and more disturbing, isomorphisms. First, like Rawls's well-ordered society, the symphony orchestra relies on a systematic rationality. Rawls's political liberalism presumes the creation of reasonable individuals, that is, responsible and responsive citizens. In Foucauldian terms, von Humboldt's *Bildungsroman* may be seen as a disciplinary micropolitics, here in musical form. In *Orchestra Speaks,* Bernard Shore characterizes the orchestra as "in the main, a patient, loyal animal" (1938, 25). He contrasts orchestral musicians' disciplined regimen with individual expression:

> As a vocation, orchestral playing cannot satisfy the craving for freedom and self-expression latent in the musicians' heart. Some excellent players will have none of it, and prefer to play unaccompanied Bach outside Queen's Hall. They are able, at least, to hear their own performances, when and where they choose, while their brothers in the orchestra may not have heard themselves play for years. Moreover, we have to make music when and where we are told! (1938, 8)

Bildung here is an aesthetic pedagogy, a technique for unifying citizens that is all too easily extended from national community to universal/ized humanity (Redfield 2003, 45). In a fascinating experiment in civic education, Venezuela recently formed a National System of Children's Orchestras. Funded by private donations and government grants, the orchestras are intended to teach "former street kids, gang members, drug users, and abused children" to play classical music (Jones 1999, 8). Jones describes the result: "Dressed in freshly laundered white shirts the youngsters file calmly into the performance hall and launch into surprisingly respectable renditions of Marc-Antoine Charpentier's 'Te Deum' and 'Hallelujah' from Handel's 'Messiah'" (1999, 8). In this example, *Bildung* reaches beyond state institutions deep into family structures; it supercedes parents' role in educating children and tries to reform those it presently deems unfit for citizenship (Redfield 2003).

The symphony orchestra combines this systematic rationality with a nineteenth-century nationalistic monoculturalism, according to Osborne (1999). Here a second parallel with Rawls's rendition of overlapping consensus emerges. Early orchestras did not use conductors, but instead relied on a player off-stage, who pounded the floor with a stick to keep the beat. Rawls's overlapping consensus also lacks an obvious composer-conductor, although an invisible hand may guide its participants. Rawls compares his well-ordered society to Smith's division of labor as well as von Humboldt's social union of social unions (1999a, 460n4). The comparison to Smith suggests that "the felt reality" of many instruments allows the players to "follow the music" (Rawls 1958, 60–61).[13] As umpire of intuition, Rawls himself seems a likely candidate for the invisible conductor-composer in the wings. Indeed, he elsewhere suggests that his *A Theory of Justice* itself become a topic of public discussion—with symphony as the orchestrated outcome, rather than cacophony or silence.[14]

The gendered quality of Rawls's metaphor also emerges more clearly here. In the mid-nineteenth century, large, amateur, orchestras began to perform public concerts for mass audiences in major European cities. These public orchestras introduced on-stage conductors as an attempt to compensate for the increased numbers and decreased expertise of their players. The music historian Denis Stevens describes their "problem of scale" with political metaphors: "The principle of government by a benevolent oligarch may work in a chamber ensemble, but in the case of a full symphony orchestra, only one solution proposes itself, and that is monarchy" (1986, 234). The first orchestral conductors were often also the composers of the musical score. They created, elicited, and sustained the emotional unity so eloquently described in the opening epigraph from Zehetner, first violinist of the Vienna Philharmonic. Not surprisingly, the conductor's baton was also a mid-nineteenth-century innovation. Bernard Shore offers this description of the legendary Toscanini's stick:

> First is the magnificent sweep . . . which seems to hold all the threads of the orchestra and to imbue them with life. Secondly, there is his not so apparent, but extraordinarily dynamic, almost magical preparation for his beats. The former holds audience and orchestra alike; in the latter only the orchestra can appreciate the wonderful anticipation of the beat. . . . It suddenly finds itself whipped up, and the whole orchestra shot with a terrific rhythmic impulse. (1938, 169)

The result is an expansive aestheticism, an experience all too easily replicated in politics.

The irony here is striking. As Andrew Hewitt notes, "individualism is a 'collective ideology of the unique,' made possible as an 'ism' by precisely that dynamic of charismatic authority, that interplay of collectivity and uniqueness, within which fascism is generated" (1993, 90). A primary purpose of Rawls's theory of justice, particularly his distinction between comprehensive doctrines and his political liberalism is, of course, to guard against just such dangers. The original position with its veil of ignorance privileges the detached observer, a third-person perspective (Dean 1996). Rawls also develops his idea of social union in tandem with basic liberties, coupling its larger social good with respect for free speech and civil disobedience. He clearly intends his "*sense* of justice" to support what George Kateb has called a "democratic aestheticism," a "receptivity or responsiveness to as much of the world as possible—its persons, its events and situations, its conditions, its patterns and sequences" (2000, 31). As we saw earlier, Kateb's democratic aesthetic requires a proper attitude—the self-conscious, self-controlled stance of the distanced, detached observer. From this perspective, aesthetic appreciation is meant to serve morality and justice, not trump them.

However, Rawls's orchestral metaphor also reveals that this democratic aesthetic is itself culturally specific.[15] In nineteenth-century aesthetics, claims to autonomous art and disinterested judgment represented the political interests of "an acculturated middle class entitling itself to speak for the national collective" (Redfield 2003, 2–3). This context recasts Connolly's claim that Rawls is "insufficiently attuned to the persistence of becoming," that he presumes the "politics of becoming is finished," ending with liberal constitutionalism (1999, 10–11). I want instead to suggest that Rawls engages in an increasingly international politics of becoming. In *The Law of Peoples,* he describes the creation of a "society of peoples," a global symphony orchestra (Rawls 1999b). Here it is worth returning to the Central American system of youth orchestras in which Lenna plays clarinet. The Mercosur Youth Symphony (2003) claims that "the Symphony Orchestra is the only institution capable *per se* of gathering a large number of personalities to accomplish a common goal at a particular time and space." They add:

> Even though we have seen significant relevance in the symphonic life in the region, we must understand that given the fact that this music is still seen as European, orchestras risk becoming more and more representative of an elite. Only by creating awareness in the youth of the universal values of this art will we be able to make it of massive appeal thus eliminating this harmful myth. (Mercosur Youth Symphony, 2003)

Fortunately, as Theodor Adorno notes in *The Sociology of Music,* "not even as so-called 'bodies of sound' are the orchestras as homogeneous as the collective of colleagues makes one believe" (1976, 116–117). Other renditions of "symphonic justice" exist, which are far more affirming of differences. Acknowledging his debt to Rawls, Connolly recasts overlapping consensus as an "ethos of engagement," involving "critical responsiveness" to the "plurovocity" of comprehensive doctrines. Daniel Dombrowski (2001) develops a more extensive argument for the compatibility of political liberalism with comprehensive doctrines. He claims that "overlapping consensus . . . allows citizens to invoke theological or metaphysical doctrines if they wish, although it is not necessary to do so to support the principle of a well-ordered society" (2001, x). A citizen can "fill out" her "justification" for political liberalism by "embedding it in some way in her comprehensive religious (or philosophical) doctrine" (2001, 85). However, Rawls would still sharply distinguish a "spiritual or interior religion" from a "political[ly] hegemonic" one. Recognizing the political dangers of "self-absorption," Dombrowski insists that "political liberals who are religious believers cultivate an inwardness that leads to the other (or better, the Other)" (2001, 160). I return to music, specifically song, as a technique for developing the spiritual/material aspects of this expansive interiority in chapter five.

A final musical example conveys the "generous ethos of engagement" Connolly associates with "plurovocity" and gives symphonic justice renewed meaning. The indigenous composer, Brent Michael Davids, questions notions of autonomous art and, with it, detached observation. He argues that "In ritual there may exist no separate category of art or music. Each artistic, musical moment of indigenous life expresses the entire world in ways particular to that specific moment, whether it be on the rez or on film" (1995). As a result, art has "vitality" only in its performance, as "the process of art-ing" or creating a world together. Others also suggest that the verb "to music," or the gerund "musiking," should replace the noun "music" to convey "the ways in which sounds themselves might enable us to articulate and to envision new forms of social organization" (Heble 2003, 236). For Davids, "self-determination" or "empowerment" are the relevant standards for musical meaning: "It is how we work out our discussions—agreements or disagreements—that is important to the meaning of music" (Davids 1995). If that process is wrong, the art—music or film—will be wrong.

Davids recently composed "PauWau: A Gathering of Nations," a symphony representing the typical events of a powwow day. Of PauWau, one music critic writes: "The idea . . . is to bring the sounds, colors, and atmosphere of the powwow into the concert hall. . . ." (Sheridan 2000, 2). To involve the audience in the performance, dancers in native dress, including bells, perform in the aisles. A chorus, wearing their everyday southwestern clothes, sings in the nasal tones of Native American vocal music. An emcee welcomes the audience, introduces Davids (a flutist), and narrates the symphony. Darrel Randel (principle oboist, New Mexico Symphony Orchestra) describes the composition: "He [Davids] uses very complicated, challenging rhythms, bringing organization to what appears to be chaos" (quoted in Sheridan 2000, 3). David Lockington, conductor of the New Mexico Symphony Orchestra, says "The repetition is such that you recognize something is coming around again, but the pattern's not obvious until you've heard it many times" (quoted in Sheridan 2000, 3). Davids's score bears the following dedication:

> In loving memory of my English Grandparents and my Mohican Grandparents, the last of which traveled to a new season in late summer of 1998. And to my very old English and Mohican relatives, the Pilgrim who Mayflowered the ocean to land on Native soil, and the Mohican who was there to meet him. (Quoted in Sheridan 2000, 4)

Perhaps most important, in the present context, Davids's narrative includes a musical quiz for the audience: "What's the definition of a grand pause?" he queries. "A grand pause is when the conductor loses his place" (quoted in Sheridan 2000, 3).

Davids's most recent composition, "Guardians of the Grand Canyon," further decenters the composer/conductor. The composition is a tribute to the Havasupai, a reclusive tribe who live in the Grand Canyon as its guardians. Mr. Rex Tralusi, a drummer and singer, says of the Havasupai, "We are a very silent people, just like the rocks that you see down below. That is our way of keeping, protecting, guarding the Grand Canyon is by being very silent" (quoted by Headlee July 4, 2000). Davids's piece centers around the "Ram Dance," created by the Havasupai to heal the canyon after they found four rams senselessly slaughtered. When Davids decided to compose the piece he walked into the canyon to talk with the Havasupai. Since they trusted him to respect their traditions, they agreed to perform the dance when the piece premiered. Davids describes his process of composition as follows:

> How do you incorporate a traditional Native song into classical music when the Havasupai don't read music and they've never really followed a conductor for music or anything like that? So, how do you give instructions? I figured if I wrote the music correctly and gave them a lot of good pitch reference and rhythm reference before they actually came in with their part, that they might be able to come in naturally, you know, in the right key and the right tempo and everything. (Quoted by Headlee July 4, 2000)

He concludes, "I don't know if that's going to work exactly, but I strongly think that it will" (quoted by Headlee July 4, 2000).

CHAPTER FOUR

Women's Music: "Singing For Our Lives"

> Being a troubadour, being an artist, being a political musician is a constant state of motion—I suppose that's where the idea of movements came from. (Holly Near quoted in Watrous and Blanchard 1990, 38)

> Whenever new ideas emerge, songs soon follow and before long the songs are leading. (Holly Near, "Grace Notes from Holly Near" 1990, 62)

Only a public discourse that extends beyond rational argument can create and sustain the vital civil society an inclusive democracy requires. "Voice as music," I argue, suggests a powerful medium of political communication employed by social movements, but so far largely unnoticed by democratic theorists. By constructing vocality in its various forms as an/Other to literacy, Habermas and Rawls typify the oral/literate paradigm of modern, Western, liberal democracy (Biakolo 1999). Embodied voice becomes an "exit" from politics rather than a legitimate form of political rhetoric (De Certeau 1996, 42). In contrast to their theories, "movement music" neither reduces citizens' voice/s to irrational cries nor translates them into public "texts"—debates, laws, polls, and votes. Instead, it employs the primal, material, and, I argue, spiritual energies of civil society in the pursuit of justice, moving back and forth, up and down, between deliberative democrats' more institutionalized politics and the visceral politics espoused by agonistic democrats. In the process, it can transform both registers.

In this chapter, I begin to explore how the music of social movements, specifically, "women's music," reestablishes the importance of orality, especially in the politics of predominately literate cultures. Lyn Mikel Brown and Carol Gilligan, who describe embodied voice/s with musical metaphors, write: "voice, because it is embodied, connects rather than separates psyche and body; because voice is in language, it also joins psyche and culture" (1992, 20). Musical language, Gilligan argues, better expresses the "harmonics of psychic life," the "orchestration of feelings," the "polyphonic nature of any utterance," and "the symbolic nature not only of what is said but also of what is *not* said" (Brown and Gilligan 1992, 23). Musical counterpoint also provides "a way to listen to many voices, as themes and variations on themes, and to correct for not listening to particular themes" (Gilligan et al 1990, 322). The music Gilligan hears is a "fugue," which weaves together two "plainsongs": the "voice/s" of men and women, with their different emphases on justice and care, rights and responsibility, separation and connection, respectively (1990, 321–322). With her musical metaphors, Gilligan suggests that second-wave feminists, so often accused of essentialism, anticipated some aspects of postmodernism. Her metaphors also point toward music of the feminist movement or "women's music" as a likely location for expressions of difference. Indeed, Alice Echols interprets Gilligan's argument for women's different voice/s as belated confirmation of the political contributions of cultural feminism (1989, 288).

For a variety of reasons, "women's music" has received little attention in existing studies of music and social movements. Simon Frith argues that the feminist movement is not "an obviously musical movement" and dismisses "women's music" as "defined ideologically," saying, "It is a category that only makes sense as an argument about 'mainstream music' as well as about women; it describes what is not included in male-dominated music of all sorts" (1996, 87). The association of "women's music" with a lesbian subculture rather than mainstream feminism may further explain the limited attention it receives. As I discuss later, lesbian-feminist musicians are often assumed to reach only their marginalized subculture. One effect may be that they face fewer social controls than heterosexual women musicians (Koskoff 1991). In other words, the power of lesbian-feminist music to challenge social norms may be related to its peripheral location and marginal status (Shepherd 1993).

Definitions of "women's music" vary as do explanations of its origins. Toni Armstong first defined it as "music by women, for women, about women, and financially controlled by women" (quoted in Lont 1992, 242). Beyond the music, it provided "a tangible example of the power of women organized apart from the dominant culture" (Lont 1992, 242). Meg Christian (one of the original four performers of "women's music," along with Margie Adam, Holly Near, and Chris Williamson) describes it as "music that honors women, that respects our special strengths, celebrates our lives, supports and validates us and teaches us" (quoted in Kort 1983, 39). According to Near, "Women's music affirms the uniqueness of what women have to say and how we want to say it" (with Derk Richardson 1990, 255).

Originating in the early 1970s, "women's music" helped implement the progressive cultural legacy of the sixties. Near writes, "The 1970s changed a lot of attitudes. People began to put the ideas to *work*, which is the next step after what was experienced as the cultural revolution of the 1960s. . . . What is this idea that it all happened in the 1960s? That kind of nostalgic interpretation of history disempowers the present and confuses one's plans for the future" (quoted in Watrous and Blanchard 1990, 36). Feminist musicians claimed roots in the antiwar and civil rights movements. They reacted against women's oppression within the New Left and lesbians' exclusion from mainstream feminism. Their concerts raised issues central to the women's movement, and bridged gaps between feminist theory and practice (Tilchen 1984, 288). Tilchen's list of these issues includes: "women-only and lesbian-only concerts; accessibility for the disabled; interpretation for the hearing-impaired; sliding scale fees and work exchange for poor women; volunteer vs. paid work; political vs. love songs; collective structures vs. capitalist methods; commercialism vs. intimacy; outreach to the mainstream vs. cultural independence; politics vs. culture . . ." (1984, 288).

Holly Near, whose music I emphasize here, has been described as the "most talented and hardest to characterize of the new feminist singers" (Rodnitsky 1975, 83). Her music is "topical," "political," and yet somehow "palatable" to "middle-America" (Tilchen 1984, 298). In this respect, her music confounds distinctions between high art and mass culture. It functions as what Eyerman and Jamison call "another kind of social theory" (1998, 138). They describe an "ongoing process of translating the political radicalism that was expressed by relatively small coteries of critical intellectuals and political activists into a much different and far more accessible idiom" (1998, 138). Other scholars suggest that political artists are not only translating, but also "creating new kinds of social theory. . . ." (Lipsitz, quoted in Heble 2003, 238). According to Lipsitz, "we have much to learn from artists who are facing up to the things that are killing them and their communities . . . Engaged in the hard work of fashioning cultural and political coalitions based on shared suffering, they have been forced to think clearly about cultural production in contemporary society" (quoted in Heble 2003, 238). Near simply claims that often the "songs are leading" the larger society. Long before "globalization" became a political topic, she brought a global perspective to "women's music." Describing Redwood Records, her worker-managed and worker-owned recording company, she says, "I think now our perceptions can be identified as a world view which combines feminism, human and civil rights, peace and justice, and global perspective, spirituality and history, as well as a vision of the future. I *believe* in all of that" (quoted in Watrous and Blanchard 1990, 36). Redwood Cultural Work, its nonprofit affiliate, has pursued cross-cultural projects that "promote peace, feminism and understanding through music" (Near with Derk Richardson 1990, 277).

A self-described "political artist" and "cultural worker," Near sings music that exemplifies the transformative power of vocal sound. Her music, I argue, illustrates four ways movement music can expand concepts of public discourse and contribute to a more inclusive, a more radical, democracy. First, and most important, it blurs the boundaries of linguistic consciousness and, with it, modern subjectivity. Second, it raises consciousness, unsettling cultural identities as it politicizes civil society. Third, it undermines the will to consensus and promotes coalition formation between different constituencies. Fourth, it engages audiences, encouraging a responsive and responsible citizenry.

"Sing To Me The Dream": Subjects and Sounds

> When you speak the language of your life/I do not know the story/The words are only sounds/That leave my mind to wonder. . . . When you sing your language I feel love/Now I know the story/The songs are mighty sounds/That fill my mind with wonder. (Holly Near, "Sing To Me The Dream")

As we have seen, deliberative democrats treat language as the primary medium through which people seek mutual understanding. Indeed, Habermas's controversial claim that people use language in similar ways rests on a distinction between linguistic and non- or prelinguistic communication. The latter includes the "gestures" and "contexts" of discourse, or its animal and oral features. Deliberative democrats often disparage these less-than-linguistic forms of communication as rhetorical strategies and/or instrumental rationality. Efforts to contain them, including attempts to translate "voice/s" into "text/s," limit deliberative democrats' ability to address the visceral register, a source of anxieties over identity and creative energies for change.

To understand how music, more specifically, song, engages this register, we need to reconsider the relationship between linguistic and musical sound. According to John Shepherd, ". . . the inherent characteristics of the *sounds* of language can have no necessary relationship to the inherent characteristics of such objects as *visually* defined" (1993, 54). Spoken language involves an arbitrary, cross-sensory—vocal/visual—relationship. With writing, even this link between subjects, sounds, and objects becomes obsolete. "Sound—ephemeral, evanescent, slippery, and challenging—ceases to be the central presence in language. It is replaced increasingly by the safety, permanence, immutability, silence, and isolation of vision" (1993, 55). Musical song, however, involves a "homology" between "the sound of evocation and reference" (1993, 50). It connects inner and outer worlds, "mapping" psychosomatic processes onto cultural ones (and vice versa). "As discursively constituted," Shepherd claims, "music can evoke and refer to, give life to, our corporeal existence" (1993, 51).[1]

This explains the power of songs through melodies and rhythms "to speak the truth without saying the [exact] words" (Near 1985, 76). Near describes a Vietnamese woman who sang her "a song in 'poet's code,' where the true meaning takes cover between the lines" (1985, 77). In prison, under torture, as protest, to identify—"The songs are sung, regardless. The songs. The songs!" (1985, 77). When words are too dangerous or in another language or from another culture, songs provide a form of "polycultural" communication.[2] Of spanning cultural differences, Near remarks, "I love how women find their way across the borders" (with Derk Richardson 1990, 128).

Near does not present music as an essentialized other which guarantees language, however. She speaks instead of the power of culture more generally—"language is like songs, like food, like dance"—to express and "undo how we think" (quoted in Watrous and Blanchard 1990, 35). In a rational/ized society, music is often dismissed as an irrational or nonrational and, hence, unimportant form of communication.[3] Yet its extra-rational quality also makes it a potentially powerful threat to the established order; voices are instruments, and songs are "willed" sound (Frith 1996, 187). The singing voice often reveals "unexplored and undesignated sites of meaning," rather than its absence (Barrett 1999, 65). Near recounts her dismay when a popular label representative decided she "wouldn't become a successful pop vocalist because there was no element of submission in [her] voice" (with Derk Richardson 1990, 79). In response, she wrote about the family ranch, the place where her voice grew strong: "I think sometimes if you're brought up in a confined space your body, your voice, your attitudes take on those environmental restrictions. There was just all this space. . . ." (1979, 12). Other studies show that music allows women, especially adolescent girls, to experience their bodies as active subjects, rather than passive objects of male desire. Singing, a tactile and aural movement between internal and external worlds, expresses "an active affirmation of self through the 'other' [text] of music" (Pegley and Caputo 1994, 304).[4]

Paradoxically, this power of song resides in its "out-of-controlledness." As moving sound, vocal song "escapes" from "a body that the mind—language—can no longer control" (Frith 1996, 192). Women involved in music have a threefold potential for "out-of-controlledness": 1) the sound properties of music converge with (2) its supernatural associations and (3) with women's sexuality, more precisely, fertility (Koskoff 1991, 776). In cultures committed to rational control over animal and spiritual powers, women's musical creations are often carefully restricted. Shepherd identifies disturbing parallels between the process of rationalizing music and objectifying women, and claims they occupy similar social spaces: "Music [like women] reaffirms the flux and concreteness of the social world at the same time that, through its categorization and packaging, it denies them" (1993, 59). Near's music taps these energies, which resist constructions of women's identities according to heterosexist norms. She writes of the power music has to blur and cross, while also respecting, boundaries: "The songs I sing are not all about me. They pass through me but they are not me. They are us" (with Derk Richardson 1990, 205). Even beyond us, "Mostly I feel the magnitude of being alive on this planet, the only one we know of that has our kind of folks on it. It is from this state of being constantly amazed that I come to my sexuality, my politics, my spirituality, my sense of humor, and my music" (with Derk Richardson 1990, 207).

Through her artistry, Near affirms not only her identity but also her mortality. On the album, *Sky Dances*, she performs the life and death of the body in time, as music. She describes its creation: "At the risk of sounding metaphysical, the project really came to me out of the heavens . . . I wanted the album to have a raw, naked quality to it . . . we don't get to improve on how we're born and how we die; it comes to us the way it comes. I wanted this record to be out on that limb" (quoted in Watrous and Blanchard 1990, 36). The musicians worked from a "state of imperfection," rehearsing only three hours before beginning to tape. The lyrics oscillate back and forth between life and death, grief and joy, continuity and change, day and night, sound and silence. Jennifer Rycenga's characterization of lesbian compositional practices helps interpret Near's performance here. Although songs narrate the "life" of an object/subject, vocal music means more than a story-about-time or even a story-in-time. For Rycenga, it is a way of "*be-ing time*": "music is life, because it inherently involves motion, perception, reflection, separation/connection, materiality, process, relationality—it is, at root, *involved*" (1994, 283–284).

Not surprisingly, listeners remember songs because they experience them—their "periodicity"—bodily. The music "scores" the lyrics, not the obverse as in poetry (Frith 1996, 181). According to Frith, songs involve "a *struggle* between verbal and musical rhetoric, between the singer and the song" (Frith 1996, 182). "Sky Dances," Near's lead song, embraces this struggle and, with it, the natural/supernatural power of song. It breaks through the boundaries of language, the "grammatical fiction" of discrete subjects and objects. Willow, women, snakes, fish, turtles, oaks, clouds, pines, seeds, water, corn—all dance as not/one in the mirror/storm of life. Rycenga names this musical experience of unformed (and nonobjectified) bodies, "panenphysicality—a neologism based on panentheism." It is the awareness that "all is matter/energy": "Music in its physicality, takes on the quality of hierophany—it reveals the sacrality of the universe (that is, its monistic side), of the particular moment/piece/voice we are hearing (that is, its particularity and pluralism—the infinitude of moments of interaction), and of itSelf (the music as matrix/mediatrix)" (1994, 281).

This musical anti/meta/physics has profound implications for modern subjectivity. It exemplifies the "deep plurality" characteristic of agonistic democracy, and an alternative to liberal secularism and religious (and other) fundamentalisms. As moving sound, music *cannot* essentialize identities (though lyrics and performers can); it cannot mark—rich/poor, male/female, black/white, gay/straight, etc.—bodies as subjects/objects. Frith claims that "Anti-essentialism is a necessary part of musical experience, a necessary consequence of music's failure to register the separations of body and mind on which 'essential' differences . . . depend" (1996, 274). Nor does this claim "essentialize" musical experience, since "to say that the *essence* of something/someone is *a verb*, a motion, change/growth, is the opposite of the reification process that is essentialism" (Rycenga 1994, 295, n. 51). The extralinguistic quality of music instead makes it a powerful medium for disrupting established notions of subjectivity.

"You Bet": Consciousness-Raising and Micropolitics

> Linger on the details,/The part that reflects the change./There lives revolution./Our everyday lives, the changes inside/Become our political songs. (Holly Near, "You Bet")

In deliberative democratic theory, social movements join the seam between lifeworld and system, creating cultural identities and influencing political institutions. In order to be heard, deliberative citizens must express their personal experiences in publicly accessible ways. For oppressed groups struggling to articulate their identities, this requirement can minimize what Orville Lee calls "the constitutive force of symbolic power." Alongside economic and political democracy, Lee advocates a "symbolic democracy," which entails "a right to cultural creation," to "the equalization of the capacity of individuals and groups to materialize (i.e., institutionalize symbolic power *beyond discourse*)" (1998, 448). Transgressive art, Lee claims, can transform the symbolic order, even the concept of symbolic order, by creating micropolitical identities continually open to new possibilities.

When asked which of her accomplishments she valued most, Near recently responded: "I continued to be changed by art and music. The people in my audience continued to write and say that they were changed" (Kupferman 2000, 9). Recognizing that what audiences hear is coded by desire, she scrambles the cultural/political codes of heterosexism. Rather than reinforce traditional sex roles, her lesbian and feminist music mediates between established and emergent identities. In his study of "micromusics," Mark Slobin describes this complex process of "codeswitching": "Subcultural musicians keep one eye on their in-group audience and the other on the superculture, looking out for useful codes and successful strategies, while a third inner eye seeks personal aesthetic satisfaction" (1993, 89). With her musical talent and training, Near could have become a Broadway star, but she refused to separate her music and politics. This has produced mixed reviews of her performances. Hal Gelb, a music critic, complains: "She criticizes the Broadway musical for 'misinformation and warped interpretations,' but opens the second act in a sequined gown slit all the way up her legs and performs a medley of belt and torch songs that goes on so long it's clear it's not wholly ironic." Near, Gelb concludes, is a "kind of Figaro, a critic of the system but not therefore automatically free of its influence" (1991, 15). Although Gelb's interpretation confirms the risk of cooptation political artists face, it mistakes or neglects Near's irony: she is an out-lesbian singing heterosexual love songs.

For Near, a lesbian love song is "*very* hard . . . to sing." With straight or mixed audiences, she feels "protective" of the lesbian community (1979, 42). She has long realized "how much the world, and even the Left, hated the fact that women loved each other" (Near 1985, 77). Through her music she celebrates a "woman culture separate and safe from patriarchal domination." By refusing to "sell" themselves through feminine stereotypes, women musicians challenge "the 'symbolic annihilation' of women and women's autonomous experiences within popular music" (Lont 1992, 242–243). At all-women concerts and women's music festivals, Near's love songs give lesbians "permission" to be "very close." Consciousness-raising here involves a different performer/audience relationship. Near writes, "we entertained . . . but we invited these women to discover their lives apart from men, to blossom in self-esteem" (with Derk Richardson 1990, 108). She hopes audiences will identify with her, and not objectify her. At her performances "an energy is born which must be sent out into the community or saved for close friends and lovers, but mustn't *all* be directed at the artist. She would be consumed by it" (1979, 42). Indeed, Near continues to be criticized for her compromises, especially for her relationships with men as well as women. Of such judgments, she writes, "In a country of 250 million people, the importance of my role in the lesbian community hit me like a tragedy" (with Derk Richardson 1990, 204).

Near also takes her lesbian feminism "into the world," reaching out to mainstream audiences through television appearances on, for example, *Sesame Street*, the *Tonight Show*, and the *Today Show*. In those contexts, she sings country and pop, songs of romance and family, to "open doors." Some feminists criticized Near's album, *How Bold*, with its "pop phrasing" and "back-up band," as "non-political" and a "sell-out" (Nash 1988, 87). She responded:

> The record was not supposed to be "political," but, in fact, I think love songs are political. The artist chooses to perpetuate certain myths . . . an evening of twenty-five I-can't-live-without-you-baby heterosexual love songs is political! For the sake of making the record accessible to a broad audience, I decided not to use pronouns. But as I began to write, I rediscovered how

> complex is the task of expressing love without falling into conventional traps. (with Derk Richardson 1990, 244)

Of "selling out" she says, "I think our [sic] kind of music belongs anywhere that it will be listened to" (quoted in Watrous and Blanchard 1990, 90). Near frequently reminds her fans: "There is compromise when you do work and when you are on the front line of any battle; it is not always pretty and comfortable and clean. I also happen to like middle America, and I have every intention to sing to them" (quoted in Watrous and Blanchard 1990, 89–91).

In two comments from a recent interview, she conveys the complexity and ambiguity of her music, its power to affirm even as it disturbs identities. She says, "Our music was an essential distributor of ideas, support, community, courage, humor and love"—and—"I like watching the unexpected, the people who go against the stereotype, who challenge convention. . . ." (Kupferman 2000, 29). Among the multiple forms of cultural expression, "what makes music special for identity—is that it defines a space without boundaries. Music is the cultural form best able both to cross borders . . . and to define places" (Frith 1996, 276). Near's performance ethic invokes this musical movement, using it to create communities and coalitions.

"We Are a Gentle, Angry People": Communities and Coalitions

> We are a gentle angry people/And we are singing, singing for our lives/We are a gentle angry people/And we are singing, singing for our lives. (Holly Near, "Singing For Our Lives")

Universal language, public discourse, overlapping consensus—deliberative democrats base their hopes for mutual understanding on the experiences they think citizens have in common. Agonistic democracy instead celebrates "dissonant conjunctions," relationships of separation/connection and identity/difference (Connolly 1999). Political coalitions exemplify one such conjunction, and movement music is an effective tactic for their formation. As an artist, Near creates three interrelated coalitions—performers, audiences, and the larger society—each of which involves a coming together without becoming the same.

Regarding the first, Near's music is multilingual, multicultural, and multigenerational. She has collaborated with singers, Meg Christian, Ronnie Gilbert, Arlo Guthrie, Pete Seeger, Mercedes Sosa, John McCutcheon; pianists, John Bucchino and Adrienne Torf; and the ensembles, Sweet Honey in the Rock, Inti Illimani, and Trapezoid. She describes her sound as "not the music of the sixties," "not exactly folk music in any traditional sense," but a "mixture of folk, pop, and musical theater" (with Derk Richardson 1990, 78). Near's concerts are also signed for the hearing-impaired, a commitment that began when her sister Timothy asked "Hol, would you like to see your songs?" Near describes ASL as a "visually poetic language" (with Derk Richardson 1990, 146). A visual language challenges standard distinctions between disembodied vision and embodied voice. Susan Bickford recently noted that visual cues—body language, facial expressions—often facilitate the interpretation of vocal messages.[5] However, she maintains that "Speaking and listening are active *responses* to each other, and they connect us in a way that no other sensory interaction does" (1996, 144). I have previously made similar arguments without recognizing how they privilege the hearing public (Love 1991). By signing/singing concerts, Near forms coalitions between deaf and other listeners, and suggests that embodying communication may matter more than the specific sense involved. This also raises questions about literal and metaphorical references to "voice" as the standard nomenclature for expressions of women's experience. Of becoming aware of her deaf listeners, Near writes: "Women often mistakenly thought that feminism was about women in one's own image" (with Derk Richardson 1990, 147).

Near's tour with Inti Illimani to protest Ronald Reagan's Central American policy further illustrates a second type of coalition: the audience. Their concerts drew audiences whose members were threatened by and even hated each other, and sometimes also "women's music." Listeners criticized the musicians for collaborating, for challenging their cultural identities: Near for working with "macho," "Latino," men; Inti for working with "a gringa and open lesbian." Of confronting these stereotypes, Near says, "With Inti . . . what was exciting was that we *don't* all agree on everything—and yet there we were, making music together, and our very diverse audiences were sitting there together in those auditoriums. And I think we have to learn to do that at every level if we're going to coexist on this planet" (quoted in Van Gelder 1985, 73).

The audience—mixed, women-only, or lesbian-only—was also an issue when Near collaborated with Bernice Johnson Reagon and Sweet Honey In The Rock, on whose music I focus in chapter five. Near and Reagon saw sexism and racism work from within to undermine the energies of their movements and to alienate potential allies. Reagon describes Sweet Honey In The Rock as "'people-identified,' which included men," and as an ensemble of "Black Woman singers" (1993a, 32). Of collaborating with Redwood, she writes, "There was clearly a Movement energy that I understood and respected" (Reagon 1993a, 33). But "being women did not prepare us for being a voice within and beyond the women's cultural network. It was culturally a White, middle-class coalition" (Reagon 1993a, 33). Working together was a trial by fire, a threat to survival. Out of it came a song about "women loving women," which, Reagon says, "scared her to death." From this experience, she formed the dual commitments to "sing about oppression of every kind, including the oppression experienced by the homosexual community" and, at the same time, to "honor private spaces" (1993, 33–34). The *Intimasphere* and, with it personal politics, takes on a new meaning here, one I explore further in chapter five.

Near's major blunders involved ". . . falling into the assumption that people from different backgrounds share a common experience," especially her ignorance of the Black church and importance of spirituals in protests (with Derk

Richardson 1990, 137). Members of the Redwood collective objected to producing a Sweet Honey record with the song "All Praise Is Due to Love" (which referred to God as He). At the time, Near took a "valid but narrow" position in support of her co-workers and a gap formed between the two organizations. Later she wrote, "I sided with my white friends out of security and familiarity more than belief. I moved too fast. I did not trust that time would take me where I needed to go. I did not hold tight to my essential belief that coalition isn't about 'taking sides'" (with Derk Richardson 1990, 139). The experience motivated her to work on her racism. She says, "I learned to sit quiet, to not always know what to do. I began to notice what freedoms of expression and movement I took for granted, avenues that were not open to people of color. And I fought to rid myself of assumptions about how people think, what people want, and where people come from. It was like learning to walk again" (with Derk Richardson 1990, 140).

A third form of coalition develops in the larger society among audiences, composers, distributors, fund-raisers, organizers, performers, reviewers, technicians, etc., associated with "women's music." Near's concerts not only create audiences that provide sites where community groups can organize. Her music also educates about feminist issues: abortion, AIDS, domestic violence, genocide, mental illness, poverty, war and peace. And, as moving sound, she intends her music to heal. "To heal" comes from the Old English, *haelen* or whole. In modern usage, it means not only "to make well," but also "to make sound"—a musical transformation (McGinnis 1980). Near writes: "For my own sake, I need to keep moving through communities and through cultures in this constant search of a holistic and inclusive politic" (quoted in Richardson 1982, 13). With this vision of wholeness, she affirms difference as a source of creativity, rather than a threat to identity (Connolly 1999, 144). When her lesbian community and the dominant culture present false choices—old vs. young, black vs. white, straight vs. gay, men vs. women, rich vs. poor, deaf vs. hearing, national vs. global—she refuses them. Of human conflict, diversity, and frailty—or politics, she writes: "Music outside of this context had no melody for my ears. We can take our differences to war or turn them into song, not a song that sounds like either of us alone, but a new song that is a coming together without either of us losing who we are" (with Derk Richardson 1990, 198). Musical coalitions, she suggests, neither resolve nor deny differences, but instead celebrate them as sources of creative energy for social change (Lorde 1984).

"Don't Let The Singer Down": Democracy and Responsibility

> All the moments are melodies/And the songs I have borrowed/They keep coming on back to me/I'm standing on shaky/common/precious ground/Filling the air with sound/Don't let the singer down. (Holly Near, "Don't Let The Singer Down")

The notion that rhetoric can further mutual understanding, as well as undermine it, seems so obvious and important that deliberative democrats' desire to free discourse from its influence is puzzling. That is, until one notices that deliberative democracy also privileges speaking over listening and performers over audiences. As one critic points out, "Communicative action does not happen in the first instance between two speakers, but between a speaker and a listener. Intersubjectivity can happen only between different subjects exercising irreducibly different modes of subjectivity" (Schweickart 1996, 317). In fact, "Speaker/audience relations" are better understood as a form of "performer/audience relations,"and both are "turn-taking relations" (Pratt 1977, 113).

Habermas's neglect of rhetoric, audiences, and listeners, for example, reflects the fear he shares with many others of an aestheticized politics. So does Rawls's attempt to orchestrate the harmonic resolution of individual and society as "symphonic justice." By limiting agency to speakers performing prescribed roles, deliberative democrats may miss the opportunity to create responsible audiences. Near embraces this challenge by distinguishing rhetorical aspects of her performances from symbolic ones. Regarding rhetoric, she questions expectations that singers be natural, be real, be sincere, on stage. Performing is artistry: "I have *learned* to be myself on stage"; "I feel that the performance is honest, and yet it's a *performance*." She puts her "whole soul" into a song in order to "manipulate" the "souls and minds" of her audience (1979, 14). She accepts this manipulative power of music and, more generally, cultural creations, as a "huge responsibility." "The power of art," she says, can "be used against a people as well as for a people. A lullaby can put a child to sleep. However, Muzak can be used to put a whole nation to sleep. Music can rouse people and inspire action. But witness the use of the brass band to call men and women to war" (with Derk Richardson 1990, 61).[6]

Near refuses to be Muzak, to sing merely to "entertain," to provide an "escape." She expects audiences to make a commitment to participate as listeners and/or singers in her concerts. Since music is "stored in the body," singing along itself becomes a form of consciousness-raising (Frith 1996, 226; Eyerman and Jamison 1998, 123). Near describes treating catcalls as challenges, not insults: "I decided that before my set was over, these whistlers would become singers, identifying rather than objectifying" (with Derk Richardson 1990, 230). She hopes the audience "walks out feeling strong because hearing songs about their lives, and the lives of other people, and hearing about struggle, and hearing about victories as well as difficulties empowers people" (1979, 14).

Empowering audiences includes "de-mystifying" herself as star, becoming "life-size," actively refusing the image of artist/prophet discussed in chapter three. Near wants "people to walk out feeling bigger than me, or as big as—that we all walk out very big together" (1979, 14). "The power of political cultural work" is to ". . . move the listener to have compassion and therefore to take action . . ." (1985, 81). Reflecting on her concerts, she says, ". . . in the end, I respect the fact that the singer leaves, but the community must stay and work it out together" (Kupferman 2000, 29).

Near locates the political power of movement music outside mainstream politics: "What political theorists and students of theory . . . need to be aware of is that to make the assumption that people who don't belong to a political party or political organization are not part of the political process, is an elitist and uninformed position" (quoted in Philipson and Omi 1984, 88). As we have seen, movement music also lies outside the mainstream recording industry. In cultural work, "politics" and "profits" pull in different directions: "art had to do with ideas, love, expression, immortality, and talent. Money had to do with the obvious material necessities" (Near with Derk Richardson 1990, 97). Women's music companies have long functioned as alternative economic institutions. According to Ginny Berson, Olivia Records (which collaborated with Redwood) "had two goals—to create an alternative economic institution which would employ women in a non-oppressive situation and to 'be in a position to affect large numbers of women'" (quoted in Lont 1992, 246). Near's autobiography documents the incredible pressure this combination put on performers; it meant continually operating near bankruptcy.[7] According to Cynthia Lont, "women's music" still receives less media (and, I would add, scholarly) attention than many other subcultural forms. Lont attributes its relative absence to the very source of its power: the association of "women's music" with the lesbian community. In the 1980s, when audiences and sales peaked, financial pressures forced performers to target mainstream audiences or build political coalitions in order to survive. Near and Redwood pursued the latter strategy for economic as well as political reasons. A second wave of "women's music" in the 1990s (whose performers include Tracy Chapman, Ani Di Franco, k.d. lang along with Phranc and 2 Nice Girls) has become more mainstream. Lont worries that major labels dilute the message of lesbian feminism, even as they broaden its reach. Although women-only artists, concerts, and festivals persist, she concedes that "the days of complete separateness from other subcultural groups is [sic] over" (Lont 1992, 253).

Without denying the continual risk of cooptation, we might also recognize this as a sign of success for the movement and its music. In this context, it seems appropriate to recall Simon Frith's description of the potential effects of music on a larger network of fixed identities:

> In taking pleasure from black or gay or female music I don't thus identify as black or gay or female (I don't actually experience these sounds as "black music" or "gay music" or "women's voices" but, rather, *participate in imagined forms of democracy and desire*, imagined forms of the social and sexual. . . . (1996, 274)

Women's Music and Musical Democracy

> Time has passed through me and become a song. I have always counted on such a song to never let me be complacent with the truth. (Holly Near with Derk Richardson, *Fire in the Rain . . . Singer in the Storm: An Autobiography* 1990, 13)

Non-essentialism, consciousness-raising, coalition-work, empowerment—these feminist concepts are not new to democratic theory. What may be new is their musical meaning, as sound in motion. This meaning remains appropriately open-ended. In our postfeminist era, some might argue that Todd Gitlin's characterization of folk in the fifties—"the living prayer of a defunct movement"—also applies to "women's music" (quoted in Eyerman and Jamison 1998, 73). Eyerman and Jamison argue that "while the political climate has moved far to the Right, the cultural climate remains open to voices of critical conscience" (1998, 73). If so, "women's music" may help "hold the place" of feminist politics. A more optimistic interpretation would stress the multiple functions musical practices continue to perform for social movements: "survival/identity, resistance/opposition, consciousness-raising/education, agitation/mobilization" Garofalo 1992, 2). Music, this list suggests, is politics, though it may be more appropriate for constituting and maintaining a political culture (what Simone Chambers calls "engendering a practice") than directly engaging with political institutions (1995, 177). In their more inclusive moments, deliberative democrats recognize the political importance of both realms as sources of community and sites of resistance.

Neither of these interpretations adequately addresses the meaning of different voice/s as musical sounds, however. It is here, I have argued, that music can contribute most to democratic theory (and that its omission from the repertoire of political communication becomes most curious). "Women's music" not only provides metaphors for democracy, but also exemplifies its practice. As moving sound, the singing voice refuses to be translated into linguistic form and, hence, it bears witness to inexpressible human suffering and provides hope for unimagined political possibilities (Heble 2003, 240–245). Near recently said, "I need you, the people out there doing this work, to pass this music on. It can do an amazing amount of work on its own if it gets out there" (Kupferman 2000, 32). In their different ways, deliberative and agonistic democrats argue that justice and injustice originate beneath established identities and institutionalized politics. If so, movement music that taps visceral responses is crucial for the creation of a more inclusive, more radical, democracy. In chapter five, I explore how music from the civil rights movement works to expand the boundaries of individual citizens as well as political institutions.

CHAPTER FIVE

Freedom Songs: Moving the Spirit

> The power of congregational singing has made tracks in my soul—I am who I am because I was raised in the shadows between the lines of my people living their lives out in a song. It really is a way to come to yourself. (Bernice Johnson Reagon, *Sweet Honey in the Rock . . . Still on the Journey* 1993b, 141)

> I looked out at the curb where the police were patrolling, and I saw one burley [sic] cop leaning back against his car singing away "Civil rights . . ." He saw me watching him, stopped abruptly, turned, and walked to the other side of the car. (Candie Carawan, quoted in Sanger 1995, 125)

> The music doesn't change governments. Some bureaucrat or some politician isn't going to be changed by some music he hears. But we can change people—individual people. The people can change governments. (Cordell Reagon, quoted in Seeger and Reiser 1989, 85)

Archaic worldviews, unmediated experiences, unreasonable doctrines, intimate disclosures, discordant voices—its prominent theorists' fears reveal the cultural limitations of deliberative democracy. For Habermas and Rawls, cries of suffering, calls for justice, must be translated into the reasonable terms of public discourse in order to protect democratic processes.

As we have seen, music—moving sound, especially, singing voice/s—threatens their modern, rational, secular, Western democracy. Although the voice of white and lesbian women carries this discursive threat, it is magnified when the singing/signing subject is black. Literacy, the sign of civilized humanity and rational subjectivity in the west, was denied to enslaved African-Americans. As Lindon Barret puts it, "The 'singing' voice challenges the primacy and exclusivity of literacy, the indomitable point of concern for Western bourgeois value whether civic, legal, or individual" (1999, 5). He adds: "In their disturbance of the already scripted significance of *signing voices* and of literacy, singing voices reopen the very issue of making *sense* in the new world" (1999, 85).

Paul Gilroy argues that the Black Atlantic world shares a "deep sense of the complicity of racial terror with reason" (1993, 73). Constructed as an/Other to white reason and its politics of literacy, Americans who are Africans have long experienced, in the familiar words of DuBois, a "double-consciousness" manifest in "two warring ideals in one dark body" (1969, 45; quoted in Monson 1996, 99). For DuBois, racism also creates a sense of "twoness" in some whites, in the "souls of them that have become painfully conscious of their whiteness; those in whose minds the paleness of their bodily skins is fraught with tremendous and eternal significance" (1910, 339; quoted in Monson 1996, 100). In a racialized culture, black and white, African- and Euro-American, are distinct but related as conflicting, intersecting, and overlapping subjects. To cast Black counter-discourses as primal and pre-modern, as embodied and entranced, is to deny this complex process of racial doubling.

A further complication arises when the counter-discourse is music, itself an/Other to language, untranslatable into written or spoken words. In *saying something, jazz improvisation and interaction*, Ingrid Monson discusses how African-American jazz musicians experience this "linguocentric predicament" as a problem of "double-consciousness *within* music" (1996, 75). Her fascinating analysis of jazz metaphors notes that the best musicians make a "horn talk," while the music of less accomplished players "isn't saying anything." Unlike Rawls's orchestral musicians with their reasonable "voice prostheses," jazz players who personify a horn refuse the separation of instrument, sound, and self. Monson also finds that the metaphor of conversation is often used to describe jazz performances. Unlike a composed musical score or text, jazz music emerges through open-ended, face-to-face interactions and includes, what Pratt called, active-listening and turn-taking. Monson proposes "conversation" to describe this discursive site potentially shared by musical and linguistic expression. Bringing processes of racial doubling together with constructs of music as an/Other, she writes: "That the verbal inventiveness of African-American speakers could be interpreted as non-verbal is highly ironic in view of the tremendous efforts undertaken by some white jazz musicians to learn how to speak as cleverly as black musicians" (Monson 1996, 91). From this perspective, "the analytic vocabulary of Western musical theory seems 'soulless'. . . ." (Monson 1996, 93).

Monson's "conversation," I would suggest, also characterizes African-American music, more broadly, from gospel choirs to blues singers, jazz ensembles, rock bands, and rap artists. Through allusions and inversions, by dissembling and signifying—African-American music says that the "unspeakable" terrors of modern reason are not "inexpressible" (Gilroy 1993, 77).[1] It speaks what Fred Moten deems "the resistance of the object," including the refusal to reproduce "the spectacular character of black suffering."[2] As he puts it: "Where shriek turns speech turns song—remote from the impossible comfort of origin—lies the trace of our descent" (Moten 2003, 22). This ancestral allusion again recalls DuBois, specifically the song lyrics found in *The Souls of Black Folks.* Of his epigraphs, DuBois writes:

> They that walked in darkness sang songs in the olden days—Sorrow Songs—for they were weary at heart. And so before each thought that I have written

> in this book I have set a phrase, a haunting echo of these weird old songs in which the soul of the black slave spoke to men. Ever since I was a child these songs have stirred me strangely. They came out of the South unknown to me, one by one, and yet at once I knew them as of me and of mine. (1969, 264)

Through their music, African-Americans supplant speech, sustain tradition, and reclaim body and soul from an oppression that refuses categorization as political, economic, or cultural, a system in which they—their people—were quite "literally" property (Gilroy 1993, 77; Barrett 1999, 79). As Holly Near and Redwood Cultural Works learned in coalition with Bernice Johnson Reagon and Sweet Honey in the Rock, African-American musical traditions present a different, a broader and deeper, challenge to democratic politics: they question the very notion of movement back and forth, up and down, between a visceral politics and politics at the level of justice. In contrast to white, middle-class, lesbian feminist claims that "the personal is political," Bernice Johnson Reagon writes, "I think everything is political. We are about being accountable" (quoted in Caraway 1991, 178). So understood, politics cannot exclude body and soul.

In this chapter, I explore how African-American freedom songs express the material/spiritual power of radical democracy.[3] I focus on three prominent features of African-American music: soul-force; improvisation; and call and response or antiphony. My examples range from slave spirituals to Motown to rap music, but I emphasize the music of Bernice Johnson Reagon and Sweet Honey in the Rock. Sweet Honey is a Washington-based a cappella sextet founded in 1973 by Reagon, one of the original Student Non-Violent Coordinating Committee (SNCC) Freedom Singers. Its members understand Sweet Honey as a collective person: "Sweet Honey is not a group, but a woman. Not an 'it' but a 'she.' Sweet Honey 'is a woman born of a struggling union of Black Woman singers'" (Davis, 2003). According to Reagon, this conviction "makes singing with Sweet Honey an ongoing experiment, a centering, expansive and unlimiting learning experience, and it makes a Sweet Honey concert a more affirming, echoing place for the human spirit moving through this widely varied world" (1993a, 38).

The music of Sweet Honey challenges existing genres, styles, and topics, including the categories of Top 40 charts. As Davis describes it, Sweet Honey "celebrates the music of the black church—spirituals, hymns and gospel—while creatively blending it with jazz, blues, R&B, pop and now rock. . . ." (2003). Recently, the rock band, Big Lovely, formed by Toshi Reagon, Bernice Johnson Reagon's daughter, has shared the stage with Sweet Honey. When Sweet Honey experienced her 30th anniversary in 2003, Bernice Johnson Reagon announced her retirement. In speaking of her decision to retire, Reagon and the members of Sweet Honey expressed their vision of leadership. In the handbill for their Washington farewell concert, Reagon wrote: "One central principle was support across generations and the notion of doing the work of your life so that you created a space not only for yourself but also for others who travel with and after you" (quoted in Davis, 2003). However, Reagon did not presume to know—or direct—what would follow: "If I left and Sweet Honey stopped because I left, that would not be my decision. . . . If I left and Sweet Honey continued after I left, that also would not be my decision" (quoted in Davis, 2003). Ysaye Barnwell, who took over directing the group, says "Leadership is something that rises and falls and rotates. . . . You become a leader when you see the need and step in. . . . I have agreed to step in" (quoted in Davis 2003). Today Sweet Honey continues the commitment of her members articulated by Reagon on the occasion of her 20th anniversary: to "embrace and celebrate [their] heritage as African American women" (Reagon 1993a, 68).

Songs and Soul-Force

> Songs were the bed of everything, and I'd never seen or felt songs do that before. (Bernice

Johnson Reagon, quoted in Seeger and Reiser, *Everybody Says Freedom* 1989, 73)

In *"When the Spirit Says Sing,"* Kerran Sanger argues that "Singing among African Americans evolved into a cultural strength because song, first, was *necessary* and, second was reinforced in the churches and in other fora for black expression" (1995, 30). Ray Pratt makes the functional connections between everyday life and political activity here even more explicit. For enslaved Africans, music served "as an instrument of expression and as an alternative way of existing—a free space fashioned out of existing materials (in this case, elements of their African cultural heritage and the new religion—the Christianity of the white man—imposed upon them)" (1994, 47). Singing was necessary for several reasons: slave traders often separated Africans who shared a common language; slave owners prohibited talk among their slaves; and southern laws made it a crime for anyone to teach a slave to read and write. This combination created extraordinarily difficult circumstances to sustain African ancestral traditions or create communities in the New World. Chants and moans, dances and gestures, rhythms and tones, became sources of collective memory and shared communication—essential tools for survival. Edouard Glissant writes: "It is nothing new to declare that for us music, gesture, dance are forms of communication, just as important as the gift of speech. This is how we first managed to emerge from the plantation . . ." (quoted in Gilroy 1993, 75).

Once enslaved Africans began to learn spoken English, overseers allowed white spirituals to be sung in the fields. Singing religious songs was thought to improve the morals of enslaved Africans and to increase their productivity. The relationship between white spirituals and slave songs raises complex questions about musical origins, including controversies over the "authenticity" of African musical traditions (Lovell 1972). I am more interested here in what Pratt calls "the process of *signification*" or "the taking of cultural elements and making them one's own completely separate from the intentions of creators" (1994, 54). As "cultural *signs,*" white spirituals were given new meanings in "slave songs": "Steal Away" announced it was time for a meeting; "The Drinking Gourd" provided directions on the underground railroad; "Sometimes I Feel Like a Motherless Child" mourned the separation of families at auction. As one slave expressed this process of transposing meanings: "Got one mind for the boss to see; got another for what I know is me" (Pratt 1994, 58). Slave spirituals functioned as means of communication, sources of information, and forms of protest among enslaved Africans. Since political realities precluded the possibility of opposition movements, music provided an effective site for cultural resistance. What DuBois called the Sorrow Songs expressed the power of a people to overcome doubt, evil, and fear, to sustain the promise of a better future. Singing was praying, and songs were prayers.

Religious worship in historically Black churches has long blurred distinctions between reading, speaking, and singing. According to Lindon Barrett,

> The [African American] vocal style, encompassing characteristics of West African traditions, is an extension of the Black preachers' style of developing sermons. Creating a cross between speech and song, the performer dramatizes his [or her] delivering with rhythmic moans, grunts, wails, shouts, glides, bends, dips, cries, hollers, vocables (words composed of various, possibly meaningless sounds), falsetto, and melodic repetition. (Maultsby quoted in Barrett 1999, 62)

Nineteenth-century white spectators often found African-American forms of religious expression confusing and disturbing, and described them as lacking in "propriety, order, significance, and meaning" (Barrett 1999, 64). In the following description of Black church services, Frederick Law Olmsted, the nineteenth-century landscape architect who designed

Central Park, draws an explicit analogy between religious and political experience:

> The *tumult* often resembled that of an *excited political meeting;* I was once surprised to find my own muscles all stretched, as if ready for a *struggle*—my face glowing and my feet stamping—having been affected *unconsciously,* as men often are, with *instinctive* bodily sympathy with the *excitement* of the crowd. (Quoted in Barrett 1999, 63)

The Reverend Wyatt T. Walker, former Executive Director, of the Southern Christian Leadership Conference (SCLC), attributes this "bodily sympathy" to the use of sound, as distinct from sight: "Black preaching, traditionally is more auditory than literary; that is, it is aimed primarily at the ear as the route to the heart as over against being aimed at the eye as the route to the mind" (1979, 23). He also notes that "A common dictum in Black church circles is 'You can't organize Black folks for anything without music'" (1979, 22).

During the civil rights movement of the sixties, African-Americans took their religious singing/praying to the streets, combining slave spirituals with topical songs from the white Left. African religious traditions remained central, especially the conviction that all of life is sacred and the commitment to bring forth the gods (Reagon 1980). Members of the movement repeatedly recount how civil rights meetings opened and closed with songs. Pete Seeger and Bob Reiser recall Dorothy Cotton, a SCLC educator/organizer: "Remembering an African tradition that the spirits will not descend until the people have sung together, she will not speak until she has brought the audience to full-throated song, to 'invoke the spirit–God or whatever, to come down and be among us'" (1989, 119). Hollis Watkins and Willie Peacock describe the freedom songs they learned at the Highlander Folk School as "organizational glue": "When you sing, you can reach deep into yourself and communicate some of what you've got to other people, and you get them to reach inside of themselves. You release your soul force, and they release theirs, until you can all feel like you are part of one great soul" (Seeger and Reiser 1989, 180). Martin Luther King perhaps said it most succinctly: singing provided a way to "meet physical force with soul force" (quoted in Sanger 1995, 153).

Along with this sense of solidarity, traditional African rhythms gave participants in the civil rights movement confidence and charisma (Spencer 1996). Bruce Hartford, a worker with the Committee on Racial Equality (CORE), testifies to the power of singing together on the March to Montgomery:

> We were singing. Somehow, I can't explain it, through the singing and the sense of our solidarity we made a kind of psychological barrier between us and the mob. Somehow we made such a wall of strength that they couldn't physically push through it to hit us with their sticks. It wasn't visual, but you could almost see our singing and our unity pushing them back. (Quoted in Seeger and Reiser 1989, 204)

Reginald Robinson, a SNCC field secretary, contrasts this powerful effect of the civil rights version of "We Shall Overcome" with its various renditions by predominantly white trade unionists:

> The tone of our "We Shall Overcome" is quite different from the way it was in union days. We put more soul in it, a sort of rocking quality, to stir one's inner feeling. You really have to experience it in action to understand the kind of power it has for us. When you get through singing it, you could walk over a bed of hot coals, and you wouldn't feel it. (Quoted by Reagon 1980, 83)

Sometimes the freedom songs not only sustained the spirits of protestors, but also created bonds with listeners. Cordell Reagon relates the following story: "A guard was beating a Freedom Rider and with blood streaming down his face, he began to sing 'We 'Shall Overcome.' The guard turned red-faced and walked away" (quoted in Reagon

1980, 83). In the epigraph, Candie Carawan describes a less violent, but similar, experience of seeing a police officer, catching and stopping himself after unwittingly joining in with protesters singing "Civil Rights." Singing, it seems, not only countered physical force, sometimes it preempted and transformed its violence.

Bernice Johnson Reagon elaborates on the singing process, which gives Black song its distinctive soul-force:

> In singing songs in a Black style, you have to be able to change the notes with feelings before the sound comes out of your body. It's like the feelings have to be inside the sound. So you are not singing notes and tones, you are giving out pieces of yourself, coming from places inside that you can only yourself visit in a singing. (1993b, 141)

She says this process of "running sound through their bodies" changes people; it creates a sense of vocal, emotional, spiritual, and physical power (1993a, 15, 60). Whether the audience is civil rights workers, the police force, or concertgoers, if they can hear more than the lyrics, then they are quite literally "moved" by their sounds. Of Sweet Honey concerts, Reagon writes "By going inside ourselves and singing specifically out of our lives, our community, and our world, we try to help those listening, in the sound of our singing to create a celebration based on what they can embrace that is real to them at that time . . ." (1993a, 37).

Reagon insists that African-Americans will not survive the next century without their music. It remains a crucial site of resistance to the oppressive conditions of a racist society, as well as a rich source of collective memory and cultural traditions. In contrast to those who lament the cooptation of African-American music, Reagon predicted a "progression of songs arising from a rich communal tradition, moving into protest forums, then to supportive concert stages, connecting with the budding folk song revival gathering steam in the Northeast, and culminating in recordings that reached national audiences throughout the 60's would occur again and again" (1983, 29). According to Fischlin, the African diaspora remains a primary source for the vast majority of "resistant musics" across the globe (2003, 25). However, rock music and concert audiences are often mistakenly dissociated from the political issues that inspire them and, hence, fall prey to "adolescent disrepute" (Fischlin 2003, 25). Today the diaspora of African music flows across the Atlantic in both directions (Gilroy 1993). Although "We Shall Overcome" was banned in South Africa under apartheid, Nelson Mandela reportedly listened to Marvin Gaye and the "sounds of Detroit" in his South African jail cell—and they comforted his soul (Gilroy 1993, 92).[4]

Improvisation

> It was the first time my living had changed a song even as it came out of my body. Freedom! (Bernice Johnson Reagon, *Sweet Honey In the Rock . . . Still On The Journey* 1993b, 154)

During a march at Albany State, Bernice Johnson Reagon was leading protesters in singing the spiritual "Over my head I see Trouble In the Air." She spontaneously changed "trouble" to "freedom," a shift that was followed by the crowd. Such improvisations were central to the oral experience of freedom songs in the civil rights movement. Traditional music—slave spirituals, gospel hymns, and trade union songs—was "moved" to address current sociopolitical issues. In his well-known typology of protest songs, R. Serge Denishoff distinguishes between two types: rhetorical and magnetic. Rhetorical songs "stressed individual indignation and dissent but did not offer a solution in a movement" (1972, 18). "Magnetic songs" instead attract "nonparticipant listener[s] to a movement or ideology." They are constructed not only to "persuade individuals, both emotionally and intellectually, into supporting and possibly joining the movement," but also to "create social cohesion or a feeling of solidarity among the membership of a social movement or specific world view" (Denishoff 1983, 5). Popular songs, often church-based, are best for accomplishing these purposes because they draw on "a commonality of experience and speed communication in terms of a perceived social discontent" (Denishoff 1983, 5). The lyrics of these familiar songs can be easily adapted or shifted as new issues arise. Wyatt Walker's remarks convey this dynamic history of songs from the civil rights movement:

> Overnight, it seems that *Freedom Songs* were born. Of course, they were not new, just revamped, and the youngsters and the oldsters of the movement had reclaimed them through an oral tradition of music that bridged the generation gap. The music of the struggle soon belonged to any sympathetic supporter of the movement. (1979, 153)

Freedom songs could be moved, led, and sung by anyone, by everyone, who had earned the right. They were simple in form, a phrase or verse sung by a songleader and followed by a group chorus. Pete Seeger contrasts this general approach with European music: "The European tradition says, Here are the notes; play it this way. The African tradition says, Here are the notes; use them as a base to improvise" (1989, 8). Wyatt Walker draws the explicit contrast between these musical styles and styles of worship: "The music of the dominant society in worship is performed within the print-oriented strictures of the melodic and harmonic discipline common to the west. Improvisation is rare in white worship, and neither is there as widespread use of choirs and congregational singing" (1979, 174). As the songs changed, so did the singers. Writing of her singing experience, Reagon says, "You can actually feel and hear the changes in your instrument and the way in which you handle a song as you sing your life" (1993b, 157).

Arguably the most famous example of protesters moving a song together is the evolution of "We Shall Overcome." Even the briefest overview of its history conveys the combined effects of black and white, rich and poor, young and old activists, while also affirming the origins of the song in black religious traditions (Reagon 1980; Sanger 1995).[5] "I'll Overcome" or "I'll Be All Right" was initially sung in black—Baptist and Methodist—churches as a gospel hymn. According to Bernice Johnson Reagon, this version of the song was widely used by the early twentieth century. In 1901, a written version of the song, "I'll Overcome Someday," was published by Charles Albert Tindley, a Black Methodist minister and composer of gospel music. However, the traditional song remained more popular with Black congregations.

In 1945, striking tobacco workers on picket lines in Charleston picked up the song and changed its first words to "We will. . . ." Although Black workers taught white union members the song, the use of music in their struggles remained "a Black domain." Reagon quotes Isiah Bennett's response when asked about the use of songs among white unionists:

> The whites would never sing. They didn't have—well, we were singing from emotion . . . mostly the white meeting they were cutting each others throats and talking about each other. . . . They never took direct action; they always wanted somebody else to do it. . . . Blacks were more emotional than whites, because we had more things to think about than whites—we had separate restrooms, we had to think about that; we had separate dining halls, we had the lowest pay, the lowest jobs, we had to think about that—we had more things on our minds. The whites were trying to make more money and better positions. That's all they had on their minds. But we had to fight the restrooms, we had to fight everything, plus the more money and more positions. (1980, 75)

In 1947, Zilphia Horton, music director at the Highlander Folk School, learned the song from some of these white union workers at a workshop. Again, Reagon quotes a personal account, from Miles Horton:

> . . . on this night she [Zilphia] said, "Have any of y'all been singing songs in your union on your picket lines?" These people didn't respond at first, so she kept pushing them. "You know you ought to have some songs down Charleston." Well they said that there was a song some of the Black people sang around and kind of changed up and made it a kind of union song. They sat down and worked on it and that night they came in with their version of "We Shall Overcome." She knew if the proper people had brought it in they could have sung it right, but these people, second hand, were kind of missing it. So she kind of worked with them on it and they learned it. Then we started singing it and it changed as it went along. (1980, 76)

Zilphia Horton later taught the song to Pete Seeger, who then taught it to Guy Carawan. After Zilphia's death, the song dropped out of Highlander history. It was resurrected by Pete Seeger when Miles Horton asked him to lead songs for a 25-year reunion.

Martin Luther King picked up the song at that reunion, and officially shifted the first line to "We Shall Overcome. . . ." In 1960, King's version became the theme of the civil rights movement and Carawan began to teach it to songleaders at Highlander workshops. Although civil rights leaders changed the key many times, they kept the song's original long meter style. In Seeger's words, the "rock-steady rhythm does not falter till the last note of the song" (Seeger and Reiser 1989, 8). Bernard Lafayette, a Mississippi freedom rider, relates the various meanings the song held for members of the movement:

> The song has different meanings at different times. Sometimes you're singing about the problems all over the world—"We Shall Overcome"; sometimes you're singing about problems in the local community—"We Shall Overcome." But in that [Montgomery] bus station it was a prayer—a song of hope that we would survive and that even

> if we in that group did not survive, then we as a people would overcome. (Quoted in Seeger and Reiser 1989, 55)

As "oral texts," freedom songs superceded the written word partly because "the oral cultural life of the community was strong, essential and, of the people" (Reagon 1980, 14). According to Reagon, "Most of the music of the world is transmitted orally. To be a master at learning and teaching music orally is to be at the center of music making in the world" (1993b, 150). Following "native oral transmission process[es]," movement songleaders played the role of ancestral "griots," "keepers of the history of African tribes—human repositories of facts, wit, and wisdom" (Ellison 1989, 5). As a movement ritual, singing "We Shall Overcome" served many purposes: it located current struggles in a larger, longer history of suffering; sustained a shared commitment to action; prompted forgiveness of adversaries; called for support from potential allies; and affirmed processes of personal and political change (Sanger 1995). Religious redemption and political emancipation converge here, and together suggest the limits of a secular democracy (Caraway 1991).

More recently, Bernice Johnson Reagon and Sweet Honey have extended African-American oral traditions to other modes of communication, including literate ones. In doing so, they join others who challenge dominant constructions of orality as an/Other to literacy, including critics of Ong's oral/literate paradigm (Biakolo 1999, Boyarin 1993). However, Reagon does not minimize the difficulty of the translation process:

> I actually have to translate my oral presentation—a "public-ation"—into what often feels like another language rather than another medium. I struggle to both respect the literary forum and at the same time push it to retain and unleash the sound of the original source, imprinted with the sound, nuance, and rhythm of my speaking voice. (2001, i)

In her preface to *We Who Believe in Freedom, Sweet Honey In The Rock . . . Still On The Journey,* Reagon writes "It seemed that in book form we could have the real Sweet Honey chorus visually heard." She thanks the contributors who "agreed to write [their] Sweet Honey melodies, rhythms, and harmonies on these pages" (1993, x–xi). One member of Sweet Honey, Tulani Jordan Kinard describes braiding hair as her "hand song"—an art she learned when she developed polyps on her vocal chords and had to be silent to heal (1993, 215). Shirley Childress Johnson, who signs Sweet Honey's concerts, describes her work as "singing in sign." She writes: "ASL is visual; it is language of the hand, the face, the body. The first language" (1993, 275, 277). These examples reinforce the claim that embodying communication matters more than the specific—literate or oral, visual or vocal—medium.[6] They also extend that argument to include more poetic and/or musical styles of writing and speaking (Salvaggio 1999). Monson's analogy with jazz improvisation, it seems, fits multiple forms of musical and linguistic conversation. My extensive quotes in this chapter reflect an effort to join—rather than disrupt—this ongoing conversation.

Call and Response

> Some voices were prettier than others and some people knew their voices better than others, but everybody had one. They just needed something to sing about. (Louise Robinson, In *Sweet Honey In the Rock . . . Still On the Journey* 1993, 98)

In her discussion of African-American congregational singing, Bernice Johnson Reagon weaves together soundings and surroundings, the movements of songs and people. Of African-Americans' journeys seeking spaces to be free, she writes: "I am talking about what you carry inside your soul, portable, going with you wherever you go. . . . More than memories, we move with sounds, ways of being . . ." (2001, 42). Those who stay in the same place can also move: "there are those people who do not leave the South for the North. The civil rights movement was grounded in those who stayed—but that they stayed does not mean they did not move. They actually moved by reorganizing the spaces they were staying in . . ." (Reagon, quoted in Davis 2003).

In congregational song tradition, this process of reorganizing interior and exterior spaces starts with "raising a song." Reagon describes it: ". . . you don't sing a song—you raise it. By offering the first line, the song leader just offers the possibility, and it is up to you individually, whether you pick it up or not. . . . It is a big personal risk" (Quoted in Seeger and Reiser, 1989, 82). Although song leaders must begin the singing, they cannot sustain or finish it. To give a song life, others must join in and through their singing move the song and themselves to a new place—with their souls intact.[7] Reagon relates the words of Deacon Reardon, a master song leader, to describe this movement of the spirit: "If you want people to be moved, let the spirit hit you, then let it go to them. Because my Bible tells me that the spirit runs from heart to heart. Strike your heart first, then mine. It'll go from me to you and from you to somebody else—that's just how it goes" (2001, 47).

Civil rights activists understood that singing had the power to move large numbers of people, and that "concerts" occurred and "stages" appeared whenever and wherever justice was at risk (Reagon 2001, 118). There were two basic types of "group participation" songs, both easy to raise, move, and recall. In the first, the song follows traditional African forms: "a phrase in two sections (A-B) [is] sung alternately by a leader and a chorus." For example, the spiritual "Certainly Lord" repeats the line "Well, have you been to the jail-" followed by "certainly Lord." In the second, the song leader gives each line of a chorus to the congregation which repeats it. "We Shall Overcome" with its leading lines that change to fit the circumstances is typical of this style (Reagon 1980, 26–27). In both types of songs, the process of singing together recognizes individual experiences and promotes group solidarity, but without resolving their different melodies into a harmonic structure. Bernice Johnson Reagon describes the relationship here between "the one and the many":

> Black American choral song style is the union of songleader and congregation: the commitment of the singers, masters of their tradition, to speak both individually and in one voice. It is an outstanding example of the unity of group statements existing in total communion with the sanctity of individual expression. (Quoted in Sanger 1995, 44)

The testimonies of civil rights activists repeatedly stress the continuity between organizers and songleaders, leaders and followers, individuals and movements. In Guy Carawan's words, "The music became a part of everything—you couldn't tell who was a singer and who was an organizer, because the organizers sang and the singers organized" (quoted in Seeger and Reiser 1989, 39). Some leaders learned to "raise" songs in church, some learned at Highlander, some were just given the gift. Bernice Johnson Reagon describes realizing how her church prepared her to lead songs: "In jail I found out that I had already been trained to lead songs, to choose songs, to teach songs. It was easy to know what song would be good to sing" (1993b, 156). Regarding the responsibility she continues to assume as a song leader, she says: "I found my voice and my stance as a fighter, and earned the right to change traditional songs to new freedom songs in the Movement" (1993b, 150).

According to Gilroy, African-American congregational singing expresses a democratic ethos that prefigures future freedoms: "There is a democratic, communitarian moment enshrined in the practice of antiphony which symbolizes and anticipates (but does not guarantee) new, non-dominating social relationships" (1993, 79). In congregational singing, no one—even the audience—is permitted to listen passively; everyone participates equally in this communal form of communication. Sweet Honey embodies this commitment to democracy in her concerts. Reagon describes concerts as ongoing conversations with the audience. The group performs without a set list with Reagon calling songs as they sing, the singers composing in concerts, in a sense, rehearsing songs as they perform them (1993a, 46). Tulani Jordan Kinard says, "Every time Bernice would call a song in concert or rehearsal the song became a living experience—a time and place in the history of our people" (1993, 211). Yasmeen, a member of Sweet Honey, describes their interaction with the audience:

> Singing is always giving and taking and giving and taking. . . . We each have our own interpretation of how we hear a song and what we mean personally regarding the words of the song. We even live the words to the songs differently from one another. . . . The listener has at least one of us she or he can relate to, which is powerful for me, and yes, we do talk to the audience while we sing, and yes, the requirement at a Sweet Honey concert (and now also at my solo performances) is that the audience responds during the singing, not only afterward. I told you—give and take. (Reagon 1993, 84)

Like Near's concert audiences, Sweet Honey performs to a diverse audience whose members from different and sometimes separate communities are joined in coalition through the singing of African-American music. A recent review describes the audience Sweet Honey creates as "a true motley, multicommunal phenomenon all its own, replete with disenfranchised hippies, tatooed denizens of the Y and X generations, 70's era feminists, and a strong, ever-growing showing of gay men and lesbians" (Tucker, 2003). Regarding her role for African-Americans, Reagon portrays Sweet Honey as "a vocal point of a community that had few geographical boundaries" (1993a, 68). In this musical community "priority is given to expressing one's own vision in a way that is not destructive, exploitative, and oppressive to others sharing the same universe" (1993a, 68). A civil rights worker, Price Cobbs conveys what this commitment to nonviolence through music produced on the March to Montgomery: "I wasn't prepared for the overwhelming feeling of love. I didn't realize that people of every color, every background, could really feel together" (quoted in Seeger and Reiser 1989, 201).

Music, Rights, and Justice

> Singing alone is not enough. . . . (Ella Baker, quoted in Seeger and Reiser, *Everybody Says Freedom* 1989, 169)

The voices of democratic citizens, I have argued, are heard not only in debates, elections, and opinions, but also through their music. For many reasons, African-Americans from slavery to civil rights to the present day have protested oppression and celebrated community by singing. Indeed, the musical diaspora that Reagon and others describe reveals the significant ways in which African-American music *is* political. Yet some scholars still argue that "music, rather than politics, has provided the real voice of black America" (Ellison 1989, 146). It is this opposition between music and politics that I continue to question. A more expansive definition of politics, which includes rhetoric and, with it, music, better accounts for the visceral reactions, the underlying energies, which animate social movements. Indeed, for oppressed groups these nondeliberative forms are often the primary, even the only, mechanisms for political communication.

In their fear of an aestheticized and, by association, irrational politics, deliberative democrats would translate the sounds of songs into arguments for justice before admitting them to public discourse. I do not deny the dangers of aestheticism in its many forms. As an expression of profundity, the material/spiritual experience of music inhabits a space itself beyond good and evil. It is human beings who bear the moral responsibility to use its power to move the spirit for democratic ends. African-American musical traditions emphatically embrace that responsibility. Soul-force, improvisation, call and response—these features celebrate democratic ideals, seeking their realization and mourning their absence. By moving the spirit, freedom songs resist the double-consciousness that marks and sustains oppression in its myriad forms. And they do so from a sense of something that is fundamentally human.

Numerous scholars have tried to describe the spirit of humanity, a fusion of posthumanist and postmodern sensibilities, found in African-American traditions. In her discussion of African-American feminists, Nancie Caraway describes their humanism as "neither foundationalist nor antifoundationalist, but extrafoundationalist" (Caraway 1991, 70). For Caraway, "lived human *gravitas* and ethical direction" must be combined with "demystifying socially constructed categories, displacing hegemonic power in the face of differences, and validating a plurality of ways of being" (1991, 71). Paul Gilroy finds a different balance point, saying the African-American musical diaspora reminds us that "communicative gestures are not expressive of an essence that exists outside of the acts which perform them and [it] thereby transmit[s] the structures of racial feeling to wider as yet uncharted worlds" (1993, 110). Of African-Americans' movements—past, present, and future—Reagon says most simply and profoundly:

> . . . sometimes as they tried to work out a way to survive in the new city, one thing they searched for was a way to keep the old songs and singing alive. At this point we are not talking about songs as music. We are also going beyond songs as singing. We are talking about what people believed you needed in order to be a whole human being. (2001, 66)

If the new world described here is to be democratic, then it is important to remember Ella Baker's words in their entirety:

> Even if segregation is gone, we will still need to be free; we will still have to see that everyone has a job. Even if we all vote, if some people are still hungry, we will not be free. . . . Singing alone is not enough. We need schools. . . . We are fighting for the freedom of the human spirit, a freedom that encompasses all mankind. (Quoted in Seeger and Rieser 1989, 169)

Although "singing alone is not enough," it remains a crucial site for symbolic resistance and a central feature of struggles for justice. Modeling herself on Sojourner Truth, Harriet Tubman, and Bessie Jones, Reagon calls herself a "singing fighter." Regarding analyses of music as merely cultural, she asks "How can you know the political, social, and economic range of a community if you don't know how they signature their identity with their soundings?" (2001, 50).[8]

In their more expansive moments democratic theorists acknowledge the visceral reactions, the cultural politics, and the personal struggles that simultaneously fuel and fight injustice. Yet reform efforts of aggregative democrats focus on institutionalized spaces, specifically electoral politics and voting rights. Deliberative democrats proposals for "autonomous and publically conducted debate" as the political complement to "the responsible assumption of one's life history" retain this separation of outer/political from inner/personal worlds (Habermas 1990, 261–262). Even agonistic democrats' "ethos of generosity" does not itself spiritualize the interactions between democratic citizens or their public discourse (Connolly 1999). The efforts of African-American "singing fighters" to "move the spirit" of a nation and its people are instructive here. To paraphrase Cordell Reagon: singing can change individuals who can then change governments (quoted in Seeger and Reiser 1989, 85). Nitanju Bolade Casel, artist, dancer, singer, and member of Sweet Honey, suggests a corresponding redefinition of the "Intimasphere" as "that close space around an individual which is sacred" and, she adds, "mine has been continually expanding over the years" (1993, 341).

CHAPTER SIX

Toward a More Musical Democracy

> An account of democracy grounded in communicative action . . . highlights the degree to which engagement is possible across the boundaries of different discourses. (John Dryzek, *Deliberative Democracy and Beyond, Liberals, Critics, Contestations* 2000, 163)

> As I grew up in a rural African American community in Southwest Georgia, the songs were everywhere. I envision that I began to learn them in the womb. (Bernice Johnson Reagon, *If You Don't Go, Don't Hinder Me* 2001, 68)

Deliberative democracy is rooted in two distinct, though related, traditions: liberal constitutionalism and critical theory (Dryzek 2000, 3). In his recent proposals for "discursive democracy," John Dryzek urges deliberative democrats to resist their tendency to privilege the former over the latter, a tendency that contributes to narrow definitions of public discourse as rational argument. This tendency only fuels critics' claims that deliberative democrats' discourse ideal is disciplinary and exclusionary, as well as restricted to politics at the level of justice. Like Young, Dryzek argues for a "more tolerant" concept of "authentic deliberation," one that includes "argument, rhetoric, humour, emotion, testimony or storytelling, and gossip" (2000,

1). However, his discursive democracy differs from Young's communicative democracy in at least two important respects. First, Dryzek places a greater emphasis on rhetoric as a medium through which citizens communicate with the state. For Dryzek, rhetorical means are not limited to a symbolic or expressive politics, to affirmations of identity and claims for recognition. Rhetoric also plays a role in substantive political decisions, including the redistribution of resources. Second, and perhaps for this reason, Dryzek is very attentive to the power of rhetoric to distort communication, to manipulate e/motions, and, hence, to coerce its audiences. He insists that rhetoric meet the same standards as so-called rational forms of public discourse; all styles of political communication must be "noncoercive" and "capable of connecting the particular to the general" (2000, 167).

With this argument, Dryzek would address deliberative democrats' fears of an aestheticized politics while simultaneously promoting the "contestation of discourses," including discursive styles. As he puts it, "rhetoric is an important mode of communication . . . because it entails communication that attempts to reach those subscribing to a different frame of reference, or discourse" (2000, 167). Yet Dryzek and other deliberative theorists who consider rhetoric in their analyses of political communication seldom include music. I have argued that this omission reflects the biases of a literate culture, a secular society, and a disembodied politics, in other words, the limitations of modern, Western, liberal concepts of democracy. Before revisiting the specific contributions of music, especially singing, to democratic discourse, I want to briefly re-turn the overdrawn opposition between aesthetics and politics with which we began.

In his discussion of rebel musics, Daniel Fischlin urges scholars to shift their focus from the aestheticization of politics to the "aesthetics of depoliticization" of music and the arts, more generally (2003, 11).[1] The reversal he proposes further illustrates why deliberative democrats do not—and cannot—avoid the dangers of an aestheticized politics by restricting public discourse to rational arguments and legal rights. Such efforts to depoliticize aesthetics merely limit the capacity of democratic theorists to recognize and resist state-sponsored cultural projects. According to Marc Redfield, liberal democratic citizens are the subjects of a political culture and, hence, the objects of an "aesthetic pedagogy" that translates and transforms difference into "unisonance" (2003, 48). An aesthetic of depoliticized art reproduces, even as it obscures, this liberal project of civic education. In doing so, it also reinforces concepts of democratic politics as an object to be consumed by its citizen-subjects, the autonomous possessors of individual rights. As Andrew Hewitt puts the point, liberal autonomy is a "collective ideology of the unique" individual (Valesia quoted in Hewitt 1993, 90).

The emergence of the aesthetic as a distinct sphere coincides not only with the securing of liberal rights by a rising middle class, but also with a gender dichotomy that reproduces its male-ordered public discourse. We have already seen how deliberative democrats tend to extrapolate from particular experiences to create a universal/ized discursive style. At the same time that state-sponsored techniques of *Bildung* were forming liberal democratic subjects capable of assuming political rights and responsibilities, high culture or autonomous art was being confined to private spaces. The "political valency" of the aesthetic is, to a great extent, produced by its presumed exclusion from liberal democratic politics (Hewitt 1993, 24). This exclusion takes the form of relegating aesthetic sensibilities to subjective or personal experiences, which are also often male-defined. These experiences are arguably masculinized in their emphasis on individual control or creativity, for example, the detached observation of Kateb's aesthetic formalism or the charismatic performance of Toscanini's legendary baton. They are personal—or personalized—to the extent that they involve private ownership, such as the tasteful acquisition of high art or the appropriate display of intimate emotions. Mass art and consumer culture, especially folk, kitsch, and pop/rock, are correspondingly feminized as lacking true "artistry," authentic "individuality," and full "rationality." Not surprisingly, a concept of the sacred as the private experience of an inner world complements these notions of artistic and individual autonomy (Henaff and Strong 2001). In the terms of liberal public discourse, woman/nature/spirit tends to function as an/Other to man/culture/reason. The "out-of-controlledness" or, at least, nonrationality, of "her" material/spiritual discourses raises the threat of regression to unmediated infantile experiences, often homoerotic ones.[2] It may also sustain a vague promise of an authentic, concrete, and specific individuality (Hewitt 1993; Love 1999; Schoolman 2001).

Although they focus their fears on an aestheticized politics, deliberative and other democratic theorists also subconsciously or, perhaps, unconsciously acknowledge the dangers posed by a depoliticized aesthetic when they employ musical metaphors to describe democratic politics. Habermas moves beyond aggregative democrats' translation of the "voice" of the people into vote counts, opinion polls, and elected officials. The citizens of his deliberative democracy engage in public discourse to articulate their basic needs, create shared meanings, and influence administrative systems. Yet they do so primarily through a textually-based process of rational argument oriented toward a political consensus, and further supported by a civil society. Although Habermas gestures toward other sounds, the cries and screams of suffering and sometimes joy that animate struggles for justice, his theory of communicative rationality too quickly translates these vocalizations into speech acts and public texts, particularly legal rights. The sounds of speech, even more, the nonverbal soundings of bodies, are ultimately too intimate, too personal, too material, too spiritual—too uncontrolled and uncontrollable—to meet the standards of his communicative rationality. They represent the contained, confined spaces of the private sphere and the autonomous individual, the liberal boundaries of his deliberative democracy.

Like Habermas, Rawls includes only rational/ized "voice/s" in his concept of public discourse. However, his overlapping consensus employs a classical and instrumental musical form to resolve the dissonant sounds of civil society. Rawlsian citizens are trained musicians, members of an orchestra, who play their different instrumental parts in a common constitutional score. Although musical experience arguably animates Rawls's principles of justice, it assumes a formal, rational, textual and, for these reasons, still culturally-specific structure. Existing tensions between the individual and society are progressively resolved into orchestrated harmony. Rawlsian "symphonic justice" reproduces the cultural assumptions of liberal democratic nation-building in nineteenth-century Europe, including its twentieth-century elaborations and extensions. And, it does so without explicitly recognizing how it too discloses a world, pursues an aesthetic-cultural project, and—were it not for philosophers as the self-appointed "guardians of rationality"—might again find itself among the "neo-tribes" (Henaff and Strong, 2001, 25; Lash 1994, 135). Even philosophy, in some respects, especially philosophy, I have argued, cannot adequately protect modern reason from the dangers of regression. Ironically, philosophical efforts to separate rational from corporeal and emotional aspects of politics may actually increase the vulnerability of democratic citizens to symbolic domination. Andrew Hewitt explicitly asks the crucial question here: "Is fascism reactionary because it aestheticizes politics, or because its own aesthetic sensibilities happen to be 'reactionary'?" (1993, 24).

For modern reason adequately to reflect on itself, including its horrors, I argue, requires aesthetic resources beyond and below, but also within, the philosophical discourses of liberal democracy, including Habermas's communicative rationality and Rawls's political liberalism. Fortunately, numerous scholars are now challenging the confinement of aesthetics to separate—private and inner—spaces and claiming its importance for ethics and politics. To varying extents, they argue that aesthetics plays a crucial role in the full development of individuality, rationality, and, hence, democratic politics.

According to Martin Leet, aesthetic experience prepares individuals for political engagement by enlarging their sense of inner freedom and, with it, their capacity to resist the violence to selfhood perpetrated by the norms of identity politics and legal justice alike. Leet's aesthetic individuality functions as a democratic bulwark against political intrusions: "To conceive of citizenship in terms of individuality and of a refusal to be brow-beaten into less thoughtful forms of political participation is to maintain the spirit of *democratic* forms of change" (2004, 135). For Pieter Duvenage, aesthetics and politics are more closely connected and more deeply engaged with one another. According to Duvenage, Habermas's distinction between world-disclosive and problem-solving language, a distinction based on their different—subjective and social, respectively—validity claims, breaks down if and when artistic creativity opens itself up to social criticism. In its larger social context, the aesthetic is no longer an/Other of reason, but it instead becomes another "voice of reason." Duvenage writes: ". . . democratic politics should be open to the disclosing power of the different voices of reason—a position that should be equally sensitive to reason giving and aesthetic world disclosure" (2003, 139). Aesthetic world disclosure, he claims, plays a crucial political role in revealing "expressive needs" and recognizing "concrete others," both of which are necessary complements to the generalized norms of institutional justice (2003, 140–141). Morton Schoolman brings these arguments for aesthetic individuality and aesthetic reason together when he calls for an "aesthetic sensibility" in politics. Unlike formal reason with its need to depict and thereby control, reality, Schoolman's aesthetic sensibility, itself an aspect of reason, remains open and responsive to life in all its diversity and mystery. It resists the tendency to identify objects, including subjects-as-objects, with their various representations and, hence, supports a politics characterized by a deep and generous pluralism, rather than mass conformity (Schoolman 2001).

These scholars and many others mention, though often only in passing, the crucial roles social movements play in developing the intersections between aesthetics, ethics, and politics. Through dance, film, music, poetry, theater, and visual arts, progressive movements continue to resist forms of symbolic domination and to pluralize styles of political communication. In doing so, these movements build bridges between micropolitical and macropolitical "arts of the self," crossing a divide that still marks much of the contemporary scholarship on aesthetics and politics. Two prominent examples, both of which I discussed earlier, illustrate the different sides of this philosophical divide. In his *Neuropolitics: Thinking, Culture, Speed*, William Connolly argues that the ethos of generosity characteristic of a deep pluralism requires changes in intra- and intersubjective e/motions. He writes, "arts of the self, micropolitics, private and public deliberations, a generous ethos of engagement, and macropolitical action are interconnected, even though valuable dissonances and resistances well up between them" (2002, 136.7). Although the self-artistry Connolly advocates is micro- and macropolitical, his chosen examples from popular films tend to emphasize the body/brain/culture networks of individual agents. So, do the more mystical or subliminal "arts"—shamanism and psychotherapy—he discusses. As Connolly's metaphor of "fugitive democracy" suggests, these micropolitical arts, at best, manage to "invade," "pervade," and "unsettle" macropolitical institutions and procedures (2002, 110.1).

In *Music and Social Movements*, Eyerman and Jamison approach the same divide, but they do so from the side of macropolitical aesthetics. They claim that "by combining culture and politics, social movements serve to reconstitute both, providing a broader political and historical context for cultural expression, and offering, in turn, the resources of culture—traditions, music, artistic expression—to the action repertoires of political struggle" (1998, 7). Among the arts, they regard music as distinctive in its capacity to transform culture at a "fundamental, existential level, helping reconstitute the structures of feeling, the cognitive codes, and the collective dispositions to act, that are culture" (1998, 173). However, Eyerman and Jamison remain vague regarding the micropolitical transformations in the self associated with the collective remobilization of cultural traditions by movement music.

A third example, which also invokes musical experience, begins to "mobilize" the connections between macro- and micropolitics more fully. In her *The Enchantment of Modern Life, Attachments, Crossings, and Ethics,* Jane Bennett emphasizes the "sonorous dimension of language" and, more broadly, sensate life. She traces the etymology of "enchantment" to the French verb, *"to sing: chanter."* "To 'en-chant'" is "to surround with song or incantation; hence, to cast a spell with sounds, to make fall under the sway of a magical refrain, to carry away on a sonorous stream" (Bennett 2001, 6). According to Bennett, moments of enchantment persist even in modern, rational societies, though without metaphysical, teleological, or other philosophical justification. Regarding discourse, she asks: "Why . . . restrict one's definition of language so that only humans can have it? Birds communicate, too, and . . . so do ants and plants. Once attention is paid to the phenomena of nonhuman languages, the sonorous and affective dimension of human speech also comes to the fore" (2001, 164). Experiences of "enchantment" create "affective affinities that move from wonder to attachment and attachment to generosity" (2001, 162). Ultimately, "Humans thus appear as essentially nonhuman as well as human, a fact that they will best sense when they are en-chanted by a refrain" (2001, 168). Although "enchantment" is a "minor chord," often obscured by "more insistent sounds of suffering," Bennett claims that "the ethical and political potential within suffering is more likely to be realized if one's attention to suffering is infused by or remixed with the en-couraging experience of wonder" (2001, 160). I am sympathetic to Bennett's project and share her sense of the primordial qualities of language, even though I emphasize different aspects of the relationship between music and democracy.

While honoring the role of enchantment as an antidote to despair, I instead focus on how musical practices work to promote a more democratic politics. The women's music of Holly Near and Redwood Cultural Works and the freedom songs of Bernice Johnson Reagon and Sweet Honey in the Rock join aesthetics, ethics, and politics, and link personal and cultural identities with political struggles for justice. Their movement music can and, I argue, should prompt political theorists to envision alternative approaches to democratic discourse. With their singing, they illustrate the importance of recognizing multiple forms of political communication—music, speech, and text—as ongoing, improvised conversations.[3] Indeed, they suggest that traditional images of public intellectuals, engaged citizens, or informed voters, whose demise are often mourned by critics of mass democracy, reflect a restricted understanding of political actors and activities. The varied movements of cultural workers, political artists, and oppositional publics call for a reconceptualization of democratic discourse, a break with the "linguistification-cum-scholarization" of discourse, produced by an all too academic democratic imagination (Goody 1993; Robbins 1990, xvi).[4] The music of progressive social movements reveals that the moving sounds of citizens' voice/s provide more than metaphors for democracy; they also model its practice.

I would like to conclude by outlining five features of the more inclusive, more radical—and more musical—democracy the movement music considered here suggests. First, in a more musical democracy, citizens would resist the tendency to fix discrete subjects as objects and, with it, to dichotomize, essentialize, and/or universalize Otherness. They would regard the diverse bodies, e/motions, languages, and sounds of human beings as, at least, potentially political. An aesthetic sensibility would infuse their politics, working from within to transform individuals and institutions. When they cannot integrate various aspects of their personal and political identities, citizens of a more musical democracy would seek to balance, not compartmentalize, them. Second, they would be conscious of bodily differences and embodied experiences, including spiritual ones. They would respect ambiguities and complexities, omissions and surprises, in cross-cultural communication. They would not expect mutual understanding in public discourse, but embrace connections beyond rational argument and sometimes even rational comprehension. Third, by forming open communities and diverse coalitions, making principled as well as strategic compromises, they would resist the resolution-as-unification of their differences. They would engage in collaborative and comprehensive struggles for all aspects—cultural, economic, and political—of justice. Fourth, they would remain the agents of politics, even when they participate as its consumers or spectators. In their various roles as leaders and followers, speakers and listeners, they would recognize and assume responsibility for changing individual and collective consciousness. Fifth, and perhaps most challenging to modern, rational, secular, Western democracy, citizens of a more musical democracy would acknowledge the spirit that moves a politics dedicated to the pursuit of justice. This spirit of humanity, a sense of profundity, blurs and crosses, defines and expands, the boundaries dividing individuals, nations, and possibly species. Literally born of a love for life, further cultivated by aesthetic experiences, and openly embraced as beyond human control or will, it is, I have argued, the most important contribution of movement music to democratic politics.[5] Whether their musical soundings animate a politics of beauty or horror is ultimately the responsibility of individual citizens in democratic societies. The more musical democracy, whose features I have explored here, promotes the ongoing creation of expansive individuals, of citizens who can move—and can be moved by—the varied voice/s of democracy.

Notes

Chapter One

1. Political scientists seldom regard music as political and studies of music from other disciplines often minimize its political features. However, there are some recent exceptions. In *Democratic Artworks, Politics and the Arts from Trilling to Dylan* (1998), Charles Hersch explores the role of literature and music in processes of political education. Eyerman and Jamison's *Music and Social Movements* (1998) brings the cultural turn to social movement theory, examining how movements use music to mobilize traditions and construct identities in their struggles for sociopolitical power. Simon Frith's *Performing Rites, On the Value of Popular Music* (1996) discusses music and community, especially the relationships between aesthetics, ethics, and identity. More explicitly political is Mark Mattern's *Acting in Concert, Music, Community, and Political Action,* a study of "community-based political action through music" (1998, 4).

The classic studies of protest music are R. Serge Denishoff's *Sing a Song of Social Significance* (1983) and John Greenway's *American Folksongs of Protest* (1953). More recent sociological studies of pop and rock, such as *Reading Pop, Approaches to Textual Analysis in Popular Music* (Middleton 2000), and *The Cambridge Companion to Pop and Rock* (Frith, et al. 2001) occasionally include discussions of political implications. Ray Pratt's earlier *Rhythm and Resistance, The Political Uses of American Popular Music* (1994) focuses specifically on political impact. There are also studies of movements and their songs, such as, Kerran Sanger's *"When the Spirit Says Sing": The Role of Freedom Songs in the Civil Rights Movement* (1995) and Fred Moten's *In the Break, The Aesthetics of the Black Radical Tradition* (2003). These studies are complemented by numerous biographies and documentaries on singer/songwriters.

2. Earlier versions of this distinction include: Cohen (1989) on liberal and participatory democracy; Dryzek (1990) on fairness and deliberation; Fishkin (1991) on representative and direct democracy; Gutmann and Thompson (1996) on procedural, constitutional, and deliberative democracy; and Young (1997) on interest-based and discourse-based democracy, and more recently, differentiated representation within deliberative institutions (Young 2000).

3. Of course, democratic theorists also mix their metaphors. The following example is a familiar mixed metaphor, in this case from an aggregative democrat. In *The Semi-Sovereign People*, Schattschneider writes that "the role of the scope of conflict in politics is so great that it makes necessary a new interpretation of the political system" (1975, 5). He makes the visual metaphor explicit: "visibility is a factor in the expanding of the scope of conflict. A democratic government lives by publicity" (1975, 16). "Scope of conflict" is associated with other visual markers, for example, scale (number of parties) and shape (pieces of a pie) and slant (mobilization of bias). Schattschneider uses fewer vocal metaphors, though the following one is well-known: "The flaw in the pluralist heaven is that the heavenly chorus sings with a strong upper-class accent. Probably about 90 percent of the people cannot get into the pressure system" (1975, 34–35).

4. Ong has been vigorously criticized for his distinction between orality and literacy, which arguably minimizes the complex interactions of reading, speaking, and writing (Boyarin 1993). I agree instead with arguments

that Ong—perhaps unconsciously—employs as well as describes an oral/literate paradigm characteristic of modern, Western societies, which limits understanding of orality except as an/Other to literacy (Biakolo 1999, 62). However, he also refuses to support simplistic interpretations of literacy as progress (Hudson 1994, 166).

5. According to Young, communicative democracy involves "an equal privileging of any forms of communicative interaction where people aim to reach understanding" (1997, 65). Young's initial examples of rhetoric—"humor, wordplay, images, figures of speech"—did not include music (1997, 71). More recently, she has recognized music and, especially song, as forms of cultural expression (2000, 91, 103).

6. Young's current distinction between cultural expression and political communication exists in some tension with her earlier argument that, at its deepest level, oppression is a cultural phenomenon, expressed in a body aesthetic (1990). In *Inclusion and Democracy,* Young takes a more institutional approach and defines her subject as "*political* exclusion and marginalization" (2000, 13). "Political activity" is "any activity whose aim is to *politicize* social or economic life, to raise questions about how society should be organized, and what actions should be taken to address problems or do justice" (2000, 163). This definition leaves the status of political artists' cultural productions unresolved.

7. In this context, it is interesting to note that Kateb does not regard reading as a sensuous experience. I return to the relationship between various senses and media, as well as orality and literacy, in later chapters.

Chapter Two

1. In his superb discussion of Habermas's aesthetics, Pieter Duvenage traces these differences to the historical

contexts of successive generations of critical theorists. Regarding the second generation, he writes: "This generation came of age in the face of revelations of Nazi atrocities, and experienced the transformations around 1968 as mature theorists. In this process Habermas's motivating concern (as a member of this generation after the devastating effects of an authoritarian tradition) was to restore, defend and radicalize the universalistic imperatives of liberal democracy, procedural rationality and modernist culture—an endeavour that made less use of aesthetic arguments than the first generation" (2003, 3).

2. Personal conversation with Stephen K. White who attributed this remark to George Kateb.

3. Thomas McCarthy suggests this notion of a continuum in his introduction to *The Philosophical Discourse of Modernity* (1987, xiii). However, he does not develop its implications for Habermas's distinction between reason and rhetoric.

4. The transfer involves an ongoing tension: metaphors cannot be replaced with literal descriptors without becoming absurd and/or untrue, that is, "man is not, literally, a wolf." Yet neither are metaphors comprehensible without some empirical associations, such as the "vulpine" features of men (Hesse 1966, 163, 160, 167). Hess distinguishes her interactive theory of metaphors from mere comparisons between things. In a comparison view "the metaphor can be replaced without remainder by an explicit, literal statement of the similarities between primary and secondary systems, in other words, by a simile." For example, "man is a wolf" could be reformulated as the simile, "man is like a wolf in that . . ." (1966, 162–163).

5. Lakoff and Johnson also treat conceptual metaphors as human universals: "Primary metaphors are part of the cognitive unconscious. We acquire them automatically and

unconsciously via the normal process of neural learning and may be unaware that we have them . . ." (1999, 56). Eugene Miller lists the following "major sources of metaphors": "the human relationships of everyday life"; "making and doing things through the arts"; "the characteristics of artifacts"; "capacities of human beings"; "subhuman activities or processes in nature"; and "mathematical relations" (1979, 157). Maria Herrera-Sobek (1994) uses Habermas's theory of communicative action to analyze how metaphors link cultural patterns and formal structures. Sander Griffioen (1991) has also analyzed Habermas's covenant metaphors as a "foundational intuition" of solidarity.

6. In stressing their structural similarities, I do not mean to ignore their differences. Most significant here, ethical codes externalize inner experience, whereas legal ones address only external behaviors. See Habermas (1996, 449–455) for a more extensive discussion.

7. For a review of research on women's voices, see: Susan Gal, "Between Speech and Silence, The Problematic of Research on Language and Gender" in *Gender at the Crossroads of Knowledge: Feminist Anthropology in the Postmodern Era,* ed. Micaela di Leonardo (Berkeley: University of California Press, 1991, 175–203). The classic source is, of course, Carol Gilligan's *In a Different Voice: Psychological Theory and Women's Development* (Cambridge: Harvard University Press, 1982). A recent example is: Janet A. Flammang, *Women's Political Voice, How Women Are Transforming the Practice and Study of Politics* (Philadelphia: Temple University Press, 1997). Patricia Hill Collins also acknowledges the metaphor in *Fighting Words, Black Women and the Search For Justice* (Minneapolis: University of Minnesota Press, 1998). She associates "voice" with "breaking silence" and "talking back," with speaking from one's knowledge and experience. Her concern is that "coming to voice in the public sphere without simultaneously coming to power in the social institutions that constitute it does little to challenge the injustices

confronting African-American women as a collectivity" (1998, 76). I agree. However, an understanding of "voice" as a musical metaphor—as the embodied power of vocal sound—broadens notions of political activity. As we see in chapter five with freedom songs from the civil rights movement, music is a potentially powerful form of "symbolic disobedience that is inseparable from political protest" (Lee 1998, 449).

8. Habermas's description of his public sphere as a "formless humanity," a "subjectively anarchic" and "objectively harmonious" order, parallels Adorno's characterization of Schoenberg's music in striking respects. It also seems significant that "voice" is curiously absent from Habermas's *The Theory of Communicative Action* (1984, 1987a), despite its frequent references to harmony and dissonance. Vocal metaphors are most prominent in his earlier and later writings, specifically, *The Structural Transformation of the Public Sphere* (1991d) and *Between Facts and Norms: Contributions to a Discourse Theory of Law and Democracy* (1996).

9. Mark Slobin uses the phrase "subcultural sounds" to refer to movement music. He urges scholars "to remake, to reevaluate, and to come to grips with the power of music as the voice of a people, however defined, marketed, analyzed, and digitally sampled that voice might be" (1993, 115).

Chapter Three

1. There continues to be some question whether Rawls is best characterized as a deliberative democrat. Gutmann and Thompson (1996) identify three forms of democratic theory: constitutional; deliberative; and procedural. Although they argue that Rawls's concept of public reason becomes more deliberative in *Political Liberalism,* they also claim that he continues to prioritize "principles

of justice" over "processes of deliberation" and, hence, is best understood as a constitutional democrat (1996, 39). As they read Rawls, the agreement on principles of justice that emerges from the original position is a result of "solitary deliberation" or a "thought experiment" (Gutmann and Thompson 1996, 37). This agreement also bypasses the application of "constitutional standards" to specific cases and abstracts from "everyday processes" of deliberation (1996, 40). However, the application of Rawls's principles, including the specifics of his deliberative process, interests me less here than the *sense* of justice that motivates his theory of justice. Rawls's musical metaphors, I argue, reveal the moral foundations of his liberalism. They also suggest that he remains a deliberative democrat, despite his relative lack of concern with actually existing discourses.

2. Rawls's association of overlapping consensus with von Humboldt's social union calls into question claims that "The idea of an overlapping consensus is Rawls's own (it seems unanticipated in the history of political theory) . . ." (Wenar 1995, 33–34).

3. Although his most prominent model for a "social union of social unions" is a symphony orchestra, Rawls insists:

> I do not wish to stress, however, the cases of art and science, and high forms of religion and art and culture. . . . Indeed the reference to games not only has the virtue of simplicity but in some ways is more appropriate. It helps to show that the primary concern is that there are many types of social union and from the perspective of political justice we are not to try to rank them in value. . . . A well-ordered society, and indeed most societies, will presumably contain countless social unions of many different kinds (1999a, 462).

4. In the following passage, Rawls clarifies his distinction between games and concerts.

> . . . it turns out that the fair division of playing time between Matthew and Luke depends on their preferences, and these in turn are connected with the instruments they wish to play. Since Matthew has a threat advantage over Luke, arising from the fact that Matthew, the trumpeter, prefers both of them playing at once to neither of them playing, whereas Luke, the pianist, prefers silence to cacophony, Matthew is allotted twenty-six evenings of play to Luke's seventeen. If the situation were reversed, the threat advantage would be with Luke. . . . But we have only to suppose that Matthew is a jazz enthusiast who plays the drums, and Luke a violinist who plays sonatas, in which case it will be fair on this analysis of Matthew to play wherever and as often as he likes, assuming as it is plausible to assume that he does not care whether Luke plays or not. Clearly something has gone wrong. What is lacking is a suitable definition of a status quo that is acceptable from a moral point of view. We cannot take various contingencies as known and individual preferences as given and expect to elucidate the concept of justice (or fairness) by theories of bargaining. The conception of the original position is designed to meet the problem of the appropriate status quo. (Rawls 1999a, 116n10)

5. Rawls draws this example from R.B. Braithwaite's *Theory of Games as a Tool for the Moral Philosopher* (1953). Braithwaite specifically limits his musical game to two players, and gives each musician two opposing options: to play or not to play. For Braithwaite, making music together, more specifically, forming a symphony orchestra, seems beyond the realm of possibility.

6. Rawls's metaphorical references to social union as symphony orchestra illustrate the continuity between his

A Theory of Justice (1999a) and *Political Liberalism* (1996). The following are complete renditions of the metaphor:

> A. As a pure case to illustrate this notion of social union, we may consider a group of musicians every one of whom could have trained himself to play equally as well as the others any instrument in the orchestra, but who each have by a kind of tacit agreement set out to perfect their skills on the one they have chosen so as to realize the powers of all in their joint performances. (Rawls 1999a, 459n4)
>
> B. To illustrate the idea of social union, consider a group of gifted musicians, all of whom have the same natural talents and who could, therefore, have learned to play equally well every instrument in the orchestra. By long training and practice they have become highly proficient on their adopted instrument, recognizing that human limitations require this; they can never be sufficiently skilled on many instruments, much less play them all at once. Thus, in this special case in which everyone's natural talents are identical, the group achieves, by a coordination of activities among peers, the same totality of capacities latent in each. But even when these natural musical gifts are not equal and differ from person to person, a similar result can be achieved provided these gifts are suitably complementary and properly coordinated. In each case, persons need one another, since it is only in active cooperation with others that any one's talents can be realized, and then in large part by the efforts of all. Only in the activities of social union can the individual be complete. (Rawls 1996, 321)

7. *Oxford English Dictionary Online*, s.v. "orchestra," http://www.dictionary.oed.com (accessed June 28, 2005).

8. Writing in the context of European fascism, Bekker expresses concern about the homogenizing effects of homophonic music: "With the arrival of the sonata, the story of the orchestra ceases to be a family chronicle. Henceforth it is no longer the story of families, of historically interesting events and certain important individualities. These families have now united for the fulfillment of the state's ideal: the modern orchestra" (1936, 38). The politics of music historians' metaphors is another fascinating study.

9. *Oxford English Dictionary Online,* s.v. "symphony" and "symphonize," http://www.dictionary.oed.com (accessed June 28, 2005).

10. Again, Rosen is helpful: "This insistence on stability at the beginning and, above all, at the end of each work allowed the classical style to create and integrate forms with a dramatic violence that the preceding Baroque style never attempted and that the Romantic style that followed preferred to leave unresolved, the musical tensions unreconciled" (1997, 76).

11. Bekker uses this phrase to describe the effects of dynamic antitheses, instrumental coloring, and thematic development in homophonic music.

12. The phrase "metaphysics as metaphor" that heads this section and expresses this point is taken from Lakoff and Johnson (1999, 14).

13. Thomas McCarthy provides a literal and philosophical rendition of this orchestrated symphony: "The political participant's desire to act on publicly justifiable grounds is refracted through the political observer's recognition of the fact of reasonable pluralism and emerges as a desire to avoid ideological controversy on fundamental matters, that is, to avoid being 'unreasonable'" (1994, 60).

14. Rawls's liberal progenitors also used symphony as a metaphor for justice and society. In *An Enquiry Concerning the Principles of Morals*, Hume writes of expressing shared sentiments: "He must here, therefore, depart from his private and particular situation, and must choose a point of view, common to him with others: He must move some universal principle of the human frame, and touch a string, to which all mankind have an accord and symphony" (section 9, part 1). "Sympathy" shares its root and meaning with symphony. Compare: "All rational beings are by nature social. They are drawn one towards another by natural affections: they unite and incorporate into families, clubs, parties, and commonwealths by mutual sympathy. As by means of the sensitive soul, our several distinct parts and members do consent towards the animal functions, and are connected in one whole: even so the several parts of these rational systems or bodies politic, by virtue of this moral or interior sense, are held together, have a fellow-feeling, do succour and protect each other and jointly co-operate towards the same end" (Berkeley, *Alciphron or the Minute Philosopher*, section 16, paragraph 52); and, "This [the legislative] is the soul that gives form, life, and unity to the commonwealth: from hence the several members have their mutual influence, sympathy, and connexion . . ." (Locke, *Treatise of Civil Government*, chapter 19, paragraph 212).

15. If other musics persist in Rawls's well-ordered society, they do so only as subunions. There may be brass ensembles, chamber orchestras, string quartets, even gospel choirs, jazz bands, and rock groups—as long as their musicians are classically trained first.

Chapter Four

1. For a more extensive discussion of how these properties of musical sound challenge notions of discrete subjects and objects, see my "Why Do The Sirens Sing?

Figuring the Feminine in *Dialectic of Enlightenment*," *Theory & Event* 3:1 (1999).

2. Mark Slobin argues that the composer Shostakovich survived in Stalinist Russia, where the poet Mandelstam perished, because "a potentially subversive message [in music] could never quite be deciphered, nor did it matter as much as a questionable poem" (1993, 114).

3. For an excellent discussion, see: Susan McClary, "Reshaping a Discipline: Musicology and Feminism in the 1990s," *Feminist Studies* 19:2 (Summer 1993): 403–422.

4. Pegley and Caputo report that singing empowers adolescent girls in at least two ways: (1) they internalize music within their bodies; (2) and, they own the music because they produce it vocally. Mabel, an African-American interviewed for the "music in everyday life" project supports their findings. Asked whether music gives her a sense of power, she responded: "It does! Because I control my voice . . . You really get inspired to hit a high note and that's power, because as the people listen they're going along with me" (Crafts et al. 1993, 76).

5. Bickford suggests that "we can think of listening as having the same structure of perception as does vision; that is, the figure-ground structure can be used to describe the other-self relationship in political listening (1996, 23). However, it is speech, which—through the motion of sound—creates an "auditory path" or "interdependent dynamic" between individuals (1996, 144). Bickford also discusses ASL, but only as an example of how visual cues can "enrich listening" (1996, 143).

6. William H. McNeill offers a fascinating and chilling discussion of military and religious uses of music and dance for "muscular bonding" in *Keeping Together In Time, Dance*

and Drill in Human History (Cambridge, MA: Harvard University Press, 1995).

7. Although Near continues to perform and record, Redwood Cultural Work closed in 1996, a victim of major cuts in NEA funding and increased costs in the record industry. In her April 1996 letter "friends of Redwood" that announced the end of their 23-year effort, Susan Freundlich wrote: "Organizations devoted to multicultural arts are especially fragile, as our survival is more often tied to tax-supported grants than that of larger institutions which have a greater percentage of annual major gifts from traditional arts patrons. The arts are the canary in the mine showing us what's being lost as the new social contract plays out."

Chapter Five

1. An example of jazz dissembling that Monson discusses at length is John Coltrane's recording of "My Favorite Things," which includes many reversals of Julie Andrew's rendition in *The Sound of Music* (1996, 108–121). Holly Near provides a comparable reversal of "Somewhere Over the Rainbow" from the *Wizard of Oz.*

2. Moten refers specifically to his refusal to reproduce Frederick Douglass's story of the beating of his Aunt Hester. Frequent representations of such passages from slave narratives, he fears, reinvoke not only the horrors of slavery but also the thrill, even pleasure, of its spectacle. Author Lorene Cary walks this fine line in *The Price of a Child*, when she relates the experiences of Mercer Gray (ne: Ginnie Pryor), an escaped slave who undertakes a speaking tour to tell predominately white audiences her story. Mercer gradually begins to talk less about her experiences and more about her listeners, less about "evil Southerners" and more about complicit Northerners (1995, 265).

3. In *If You Don't Go, Don't Hinder Me* (2001), Bernice Johnson Reagon discusses the distinct features of gospel, congregational song, spirituals, and freedom songs in the history of African-American sacred song. Although differences between these genres are important, I am more interested here in shared features of African-American music, including their intersections with Euro-American musical forms. Pratt argues that African-American music shares the following features: *"percussive performance style"; "propensity for multiple meter"; "overlapping call and response"; "inner pulse control"; "suspended accentuation patterning"; "songs and dances of social allusion"* (1994, 49). Lovell (1972) provides what is regarded as the definitive discussion of the complex relationships between white and African spirituals.

4. "We Shall Overcome" is now widely sung in post-apartheid South Africa. (Information from Penny Grimbeek, a guide out of Capetown, relayed to me by a colleague, Susan Boardman.)

5. The copyright history of "We Shall Overcome" is a fascinating and troubling story in its own right. Bernice Johnson Reagon concludes her discussion with the following comment:

> Review of the copyright history reveals severe shortsightedness in the 1963 copyright. There can be found no acknowledgment of the fact that it was Blacks who had interpreted this song in a socio-political context in Charleston and Winston-Salem before it came to Zilphia Horton at Highlander. It was Blacks again in the sixties who utilized the song functionally and musically in such a way and with such power that its value as a commercial product would warrant copyright considerations. . . . (1980, 85–87)

6. Gilroy also discusses the importance of mimesis, gesture, kinesis, and costume, as additional aspects of musical performances (1993, 79).

7. In *If You Don't Go, Don't Hinder Me*, Reagon discusses Nell Irwin Painter's concept of "soul murder": the "cost that is paid when one is abused, raped, beaten, and repeatedly violated. Even if you survive the violence, there is a way in which your soul can be distorted or destroyed" (2001, 125).

8. Angela Davis notes that "black feminist traditions tend to exclude ideas produced by and within poor and working class communities, where women historically have not had the means or access to publish written texts. But some poor black women did have access to publishers of *oral* texts. In fact, in the 1920s, many black women were sought after—and often exploited by burgeoning record companies" (1998, xi).

Chapter Six

1. According to Fischlin, the depoliticizing of music, in particular, poses a dual threat to democratic politics: 1) written words may break their ties to the "sonic forces" they represent; 2) and, music and other arts may become isolated from other sites of resistance (2003, 10).

2. Redfield explicitly discusses homoerotic aspects of "the aesthetic national body" (2003, chapter 2), but they remain implicit in McNeill's discussion of "muscular bonding" in military drill (1995) and Zehetner's experience of masculine emotional unity when performing a Mahler symphony (Osborne 1999).

3. Drawing on Rousseau's philosophy, Lydia Goehr argues that words are musical; they have inflection, accent, rhythm. She concludes that "To preserve the vigour of language . . . we should try to read as we speak, not speak as we read (1998, 103).

4. Connolly explicitly acknowledges that *"intellectualism is constitutively insufficient to ethics"* and defends the "'unthought,'" which "consists of energetic assemblages that are non- or minimally ideational . . . " (2002, 110). It seems the gap between micro- and macropolitical arts of the self may partly reflect a scholarly reluctance to "acknowledge acknowledging" the intellectual norms that limit our capacity for embodied resistance (Leet 2004, 30).

5. If the future holds a "world of movement without borders," then the power of music to mobilize connections between species and nations may become increasingly important (Tarrow 1998, xi).

References

Adorno, Theodor. 1976. *The Sociology of Music*. New York: Seabury Press.

——— and Max Horkheimer. 1972. *Dialectic of Enlightenment*. Trans. John Cumming. New York: Seabury Press.

Almond, Gabriel A. and Sidney Verba, eds. 1980. *The Civic Culture Revisited, An Analytic Study*. Boston: Little, Brown.

———. 1989. *The Civic Culture: Political Attitudes and Democracy in Five Nations*. Newbury Park, CA: Sage Publications.

Attali, Jacques. 1992. *Noise, The Political Economy of Music*. Trans. Brian Massumi. Minneapolis: University of Minnesota Press.

Barrett, Lindon. 1999. *Blackness and Value, Seeing Double*. Cambridge, UK: Cambridge University Press.

Beck, Ulrich, Anthony Giddens and Scott Lash, eds. 1994. *Reflexive Modernization, Politics, Tradition and Aesthetics in the Modern Social Order*. Stanford, CA: Stanford University Press.

Bekker, Paul. 1936. *The Story of the Orchestra*. New York: W.W. Norton & Co.

Benhabib, Seyla. 1986. *Critique, Norm, and Utopia: A Study of the Foundations of Critical Theory*. New York: Columbia University Press.

Bennett, Jane. 2001. *The Enchantment of Modern Life: Attachments, Crossings, and Ethics.* Princeton, NJ: Princeton University Press.

Berkeley, George. 1990. *Alciphron: or the Minute Philosopher. On Locke, Berkeley, and Hume.* CD-ROM. Pittsboro, NC: Intelex Corporation.

Bessman, Jim. Feb. 16, 2002. Sweet Honey's Reagon follows path of the 'Singing Fighters'. *Billboard, New York* 114 (7): 38.

Biakolo, Emevwo. 1999. On the theoretical foundations of orality and literacy. *Research in African Literatures* 30 (2): 42–63.

Bickford, Susan. 1996. *The Dissonance of Democracy: Listening, Conflict, and Citizenship.* Ithaca: Cornell University Press.

Bohman, James. 1990. Communication, Ideology, and Democratic Theory. *American Political Science Review* 84(1): 93–109.

Borradori, Giovanna. 2003. *Philosophy In A Time of Terror, Dialogues With Jürgen Habermas and Jacques Derrida.* Chicago: University of Chicago Press.

Boyarin, Jonathan, ed. 1993. *The Ethnography of Reading.* Berkeley: University of California Press.

Braithwaite, R.B. 1955. *A Theory of Games as a Tool for the Moral Philosopher, An Inaugural Lecture delivered in Cambridge on 2 December 1954.* Cambridge, UK: Cambridge University Press.

Brown, Lyn Mikel, and Carol Gilligan, eds. 1992. *Meeting at the crossroads: Women's psychology and girls' development.* New York: Ballantine Books.

Brown, Wendy. 1995. *States of Injury: Power and Freedom in Late Modernity.* Princeton, NJ: Princeton University Press.

Burke, Kenneth. 1969. *A Grammar of Motives.* Berkeley: University of California Press.

Carawan, Guy, and Candie Carawan, eds. 1990. *The Story of the Civil Rights Movement Through Its Songs.* Bethlehem, PA: Sing Out Corporation.

Caraway, Nancie. 1991. *Segregated Sisterhood, Racism and the Politics of American Feminism.* Knoxville: University of Tennessee Press.

Cary, Lorene. 1995. *The Price of a Child.* New York: Vintage Books.

Casel, Nitanjy Bolade. 1993. Casserole For Life. In *Sweet Honey in the Rock . . . Still on the Journey*, ed. Bernice Johnson Reagon and Sweet Honey in the Rock. New York: Doubleday.

Chambers, Simone. 1995. Feminist Discourse/Practical Discourse. In *Feminists Read Habermas*, ed. Johanna Meehan. New York: Routledge.

Christian, Meg. 1974. The muses of Olivia: Our own economy, our own song. *Off Our Backs* (August/September): 2–3.

Cohen, Joshua. 1989. Deliberation and democratic legitimacy. In *The Good Polity, Normative Analysis of the State,* eds. Alan Hamlin and Philip Pettit. Oxford: Basil Blackwell, Ltd.

Coles, Romand. 1997. *Rethinking Generosity: Critical Theory and the Politics of Caritas.* Ithaca: Cornell University Press.

Collins, Patricia Hill. 1998. *Fighting Words, Black Women and the Search for Justice.* Minneapolis: University of Minnesota Press.

Coltrane, John. 1960. *My Favorite Things.* New York: Atlantic SD1361.

Connolly, William E. 1999. *Why I Am Not a Secularist.* Minneapolis: University of Minnesota Press.

———. 2002. *Neuropolitics: Thinking, Culture, Speed.* Minneapolis: University of Minnesota Press.

Crafts, Susan D., Daniel Cavicchi, Charles Keil, and the Music in Daily Life Project, eds. 1993. *My Music.* Hanover, NH: The University Press of New England.

Davids, Brent Michael. March 9, 1995. Indian actors are not enough; Indigenous composers empower Native films. *Indian Country Today* 14(37): C-8.

Davis, Angela Y. 1998. *Blues Legacies and Black Feminism, Gertude 'Ma' Rainey, Bessie Smith, and Billie Holiday.* New York: Pantheon Books.

Davis, Marcia. Nov. 23, 2003. Sweet Honey Loses Its Queen Bee; Bernice Johnson Reagon Retiring After 30 Years. *The Washington Post.*

Dean, Jodi. 1996. *Solidarity of Strangers: Feminism After Identity Politics.* Berkeley: University of California Press.

De Certeau, Michel. 1996. Vocal Utopias: Glossolalias. *Representations* 56 (Fall): 29–47.

———. 1997. *The Capture of Speech and Other Political Writings.* Trans. Tom Conley. Minneapolis: University of Minnesota Press.

Denisoff, Serge R. 1983. *Sing a Song of Social Significance.* Bowling Green, OH: Bowling Green State University Popular Press.

——— and Richard A. Peterson, ed. 1972. *The Sounds of Social Change, Studies in Popular Culture.* Chicago: Rand McNally.

Doherty, Lillian Eileen. 1995. Sirens, Muses, and Female Narrators in the Odyssey. In *The Distaff Side: Representing the Female in Homer's Odyssey*, ed. Beth Cohen. New York: Oxford University Press.

Dombrowski, Daniel A. 2001. *Rawls and Religion, The Case for Political Liberalism.* Albany: State University of New York Press.

"Don't Let The Singer Down," from Holly Near's *Early Warnings,* Appleseed Records 1056, © 2001, CD.

Words by Holly Near. Music by Jeff Langley. Copyright 1984 Hereford Music (ASCAP).

Dryzek, John. 1990. *Discursive Democracy, Politics, Policy, and Political Science.* New York: Cambridge University Press.

———. 2000. *Deliberative Democracy and Beyond, Liberals, Critics, Contestations.* New York: Oxford University Press.

DuBois, W.E.B. 1910. The Souls of White Folks. *Independent* 69 (August 18): 339–342.

———. 1969. *The Souls of Black Folks.* Originally published 1903. New York: New American Library

Dumm, Thomas L. 1996. *Michel Foucault and the Politics of Freedom.* Thousand Oaks, CA: Sage Publications.

Dunn, Leslie C., and Nancy A. Jones, eds. 1994. *Embodied Voices: Representing female vocality in Western culture.* Cambridge, UK: Cambridge University Press.

Dunson, Josh. 1965. *Freedom In The Air, Song Movements of the Sixties.* New York: International Publishers.

Durham, Jimmy, and Roy Brown. 1989. *Sky Dances.* Holly Near. Redwood Records.

Duvenage, Pieter. 2003. *Habermas and Aesthetics, The Limits of Communicative Reason.* Cambridge, UK: Polity Press.

Echols, Alice. 1989. *Daring to Be Bad: Radical feminism in America 1967–1975.* Minneapolis: University of Minnesota.

Ellison, Mary. 1989. *Lyrical Protest, Black Music's Struggle Against Discrimination.* New York: Praeger Publishers.

Engh, Barbara. 1993. Loving it: Music and Criticism in Roland Barthes. In *Musicology and Difference: Gender and Sexuality in Music Scholarship*, ed. Ruth A. Solie. Berkeley: University of California Press.

Eyerman, Ron, and Andrew Jamison. 1998. *Music and Social Movements: Mobilizing Traditions in the Twentieth Century*. Cambridge, UK: Cambridge University Press.

Fischlin, Daniel. 2003. Take One/Rebel Musics: Human Rights, Resistant Sounds, and the Politics of Music Making. In Daniel Fischlin and Ajay Heble, eds. *Rebel Musics, Human Rights, Resistant Sounds, and the Politics of Music Making*. Montreal, Canada: Black Rose Books.

Fishkin, James S. 1991. *Democracy and Deliberation: New Directions for Democratic Reform*. New Haven, CT: Yale University Press.

Flammang, Janet. 1997. *Women's Political Voice: How Women are Transforming the Practice and Study of Politics*. Philadelphia: Temple University Press.

Foucault, Michel. 1980. *Power/Knowledge: Selected Interviews and Other Writings, 1972–1977,* ed. Colin Gordon. New York: Pantheon Books.

Fraser, Nancy. 1997. *Justice Interruptus, Critical Reflections on the "Postsocialist" Condition.* New York: Routledge.

Freundlich, Susan. Letter to author. April 1996. Letter to friends of Redwood.

Frith, Simon. 1996. *Performing Rites: On the Value of Popular Music.* Cambridge, MA: Harvard University Press.

———. 2001. The Popular Music Industry. In *The Cambridge Companion To Pop and Rock,* eds. Simon Frith, Will Straw, and John Street. Cambridge, UK: Cambridge University Press.

Gal, Susan. 1991. Between Speech and Silence, The Problematics of Research on Language and Gender. In *Gender at the Crossroads of Knowledge: Feminist Anthropology in the Postmodern Era*, ed. Micaela di Leonardo. Berkeley: University of California Press.

Garofalo, Reebee. 1992. Introduction to *Rockin' the Boat: Mass Music and Mass Movements.* Boston: South End Press.

Gelb, Hal. 1991. Theater. *The Nation.* 11 September, 313–315.

Gilligan, Carol. 1982. *In a Different Voice: Psychological Theory and Women's Development.* Cambridge, MA: Harvard University Press.

———, Annie Rogers, and Lyn Mikel Brown. 1990. Soundings into development. In *Making Connections: The Relational Worlds of Adolescent Girls at Emma Willard School,* eds. Carol Gilligan, Nona P. Lyons, and Trudy J. Hammer. Cambridge, MA: Harvard University Press.

Gilroy, Paul. 1993. *The Black Atlantic: Modernity and Double Consciousness.* Cambridge, MA: Harvard University Press.

Goehr, Lydia. 1998. *The Quest for Voice, On Music, Politics, and the Limits of Philosophy, The 1997 Ernest Bloch Lectures.* Berkeley: University of California Press.

Goldberger, Nancy Rule, Jill M. Tarule, Blynche Clinchy, and Mary F. Belenky, eds. 1996. *Knowledge, Difference, and Power: Essays Inspired by Women's Ways of Knowing.* New York: Basic Books.

Goody, Jack R. 1993. Alternative Paths to Knowledge in Oral and Literate Cultures. In *Spoken and Written Language: Exploring Orality and Literacy,* ed. Deborah Tannen. Norwood, NJ: Ablex Publishing.

Greenway, John. 1953. *American Folksongs of Protest.* Philadelphia: University of Pennsylvania Press.

Griffioen, Sander. 1991. The Metaphor of the Covenant in Habermas. *Faith and Philosophy* 8(4): 524–560.

Gutmann, Amy, and Dennis Thompson. 1996. *Democracy and Disagreement.* Cambridge, MA: Harvard University Press.

Habermas, Jürgen. 1970a. On Systematically Distorted Communication. *Inquiry* 13: 205–218.

———. 1970b. Towards a Theory of Communicative Competence. *Inquiry* 13: 360–375.

———. 1979a. Moral Development and Ego Identity. In *Communication and the Evolution of Society*. Trans. Thomas McCarthy. Boston: Beacon Press.

———. 1979b. Towards a Reconstruction of Historical Materialism. In *Communication and the Evolution of Society*. Trans. Thomas McCarthy. Boston: Beacon Press.

———. 1984. *The Theory of Communicative Action*. Vol. 1. *Reason and the Rationalization of Society*. Trans. Thomas McCarthy. Boston: Beacon Press.

———. 1985a. *Philosophical-Political Profiles*. Trans. Frederick Lawrence. Cambridge, MA: MIT Press.

———. 1985b. On the Distinction between Poetic and Communicative Uses of Language. In *On the Pragmatics of Communication*. Ed. Maeve Cooke. Cambridge, MA: MIT Press, 1998.

———. 1985c. Questions and Counterquestions. In *On The Pragmatics of Communication*. Ed. Maeve Cooke. Cambridge, MA: MIT Press, 1998.

———. 1986. *Autonomy and Solidarity, Interviews with Jürgen Habermas*. Ed. Peter Dews. New York: Verso.

———. 1987a. *The Theory of Communicative Action*. Vol. 2. *Lifeworld and System: A Critique of Functionalist Reason*. Trans. Thomas McCarthy. Boston: Beacon Press.

———. 1987b. On Levelling the Genre Distinction Between Philosophy and Literature. In *The Philosophical Discourse of Modernity*. Trans. Frederick Lawrence. Cambridge, MA: MIT Press.

———. 1989–1990. Justice and Solidarity: On the Discussion Concerning “Stage 6.” *The Philosophical Forum* 21(1–2): 32–52.

———. 1990. Historical Consciousness and Post-Traditional Identity: The Federal Republic's Orientation to the West. In *The New Conservatism: Cultural Criticism and the Historians' Debate*. Ed. and trans. Shierry Weber Nicholsen. Cambridge, MA: MIT Press.

———. 1991a. Discourse Ethics: Notes on a Program of Philosophical Justification. In *Moral Consciousness and Communicative Action*. Trans. Christian Lenhardt and Shierry Weber Nicholsen. Cambridge, MA: MIT Press.

———. 1991b. Moral Consciousness and Communicative Action. In *Moral Consciousness and Communicative Action*.

———. 1991c. Morality and Ethical Life: Does Hegel's Critique of Kant Apply to Discourse Ethics? In *Moral Consciousness and Communicative Action.*

———. 1991d. *The Structural Transformation of the Public Sphere, An Inquiry into a Category of Bourgeois Society*. Trans. Thomas Burger with Frederick Lawrence. Cambridge, MA: MIT Press.

———. 1994. The Burdens of The Double Past. *Dissent* 41(4): 513–517.

———. 1995. Reconciliation Through the Public Use of Reason: Remarks on John Rawls's Political Liberalism. *The Journal of Philosophy* XCII (March): 109–131.

———. 1996. *Between Facts and Norms: Contributions to a Discourse Theory of Law and Democracy*. Trans. William Rehg. Cambridge, MA: MIT Press.

———. 1997. "A Conversation About Questions of Political Theory." In *A Berlin Republic: Writings on Germany*. Trans. Steven Rendall. Lincoln: University of Nebraska Press.

———. 2002. *Religion and Rationality, Essays on Reason, God, and Morality*. Ed. By Eduardo Mendieta. Cambridge, MA: MIT Press.

———. 2003. *The Future of Human Nature.* Cambridge, UK: Polity Press.

Harrell, Jean Gabbert. 1992. *Profundity: A Universal Value.* University Park, PA: Penn State Press.

Headlee, Celeste. July 4, 2000. Profile: Composer Creates Song About the Grand Canyon For Yearly Celebration. *NPR: Morning Edition*, pg. 1 (transcript).

Heble, Ajay. 2003. Take Two/Rebel Musics: Human Rights, Resistant Sounds, and the Politics of Music Making. In *Rebel Musics, Human Rights, Resistant Sounds, and the Politics of Music Making*, eds. Daniel Fischlin, and Ajay Heble. Montreal, Canada: Black Rose Books.

Henaff, Marcel and Tracy B. Strong. 2001. The Conditions of Public Space: Vision, Speech, and Theatricality. In *Public Space and Democracy*, eds. Marcel Henaff and Tracy B. Strong. Minneapolis: University of Minnesota Press.

Herrera-Sobek, Maria. 1994. Gender and rhetorical strategies in Mexican ballads and songs: plant and mineral metaphors. *Lore and Language: The Journal of the Centre for English Cultural Tradition and Language*, 12:1–2, 97–113.

Hersch, Charles. 1998. *Democratic Artworks: Politics and the Arts from Trilling to Dylan.* Albany: State University of New York Press.

Hesse, Mary B. 1966. *Models and Analogies in Science.* Notre Dame, IN: University of Notre Dame Press.

Hewitt, Andrew. 1993. *Fascist Modernism, Aesthetics, Politics, and the Avant-Garde.* Stanford, CA: Stanford University Press.

Holly Near Biography. 2002. Retrieved 16 April 2002 from the World Wide Web: http://www.hollynear.com/bio.html.

Honig, Bonnie. 1993. *Political Theory and the Displacement of Politics*. Ithaca: Cornell University Press.

Hudson, Nicholas. 1994. *Writing and European Thought*. Cambridge, UK: Cambridge University Press.

Hume, David. 1990. *An Enquiry Concerning the Principles of Morals. On Locke, Berkeley, and Hume*. CD-ROM. Pittsboro, NC: Intelex Corporation.

Johnson, Mark, ed. 1981. *Philosophical Perspectives on Metaphor*. Minneapolis: University of Minnesota Press.

Johnson, Shirley Childress. 1993. The Power of Sign. In *Sweet Honey in the Rock . . . Still on the Journey*, ed. Bernice Johnson Reagon and Sweet Honey in the Rock. New York: Doubleday.

Jones, Bart. 1999. Street Kids Discover New Life in Music: Venezuela: Organizers of children's orchestras assembled a symphony with some of the country's most troubled and abused children. Its success has been remarkable. *The Los Angeles Times* (October 31): 8.

Kateb, George. 2000. Aestheticism and Morality: Their Cooperation and Hostility. *Political Theory* 28(1): 5–37.

Kelly, George Armstrong. 1996. Veils: The Poetics of John Rawls. *Journal of the History of Ideas* 57:343–364.

Kinard, Tulani Jordan. 1993. "So Glad I'm Saved." In *Sweet Honey in the Rock . . . Still on the Journey,* ed. Bernice Johnson Reagon and Sweet Honey in the Rock. New York: Doubleday.

Klosko, George. 1997. Political Constructivism in Rawls's Political Liberalism. *American Political Science Review* 91(3): 535–546.

Kort, Michelle. 1983. Sisterhood is Profitable. *Mother Jones* (July): 39–44.

Koskoff, Ellen. 1991. *Gender, Power, and Music*. Vol. 3, *The Musical Woman: An International Perspective*. Westport, CT: Greenwood Press.

Kupferman, Wendy. 2000. Holly Near Talks About Feminism, Women's Music, Past and Present. *Sojourner: The Women's Forum* (December): 29–32.

Lakoff, George. 2002. *Moral Politics, How Liberals and Conservatives Think*. 2nd Ed. Chicago: University of Chicago Press.

——— and Mark Johnson. 1999. *Philosophy in the Flesh: The Embodied Mind and its Challenge to Western Thought.* New York: Basic Books.

Landes, Joan. 1995. The Public and the Private Sphere: A Feminist Reconstruction. In *Feminists read Habermas,* ed. Johanna Meehan. New York: Routledge.

Langley, Jeff, and Ginger Sarber. 1976. "You Can Know All I Am." Holly Near. Redwood Records.

Lash, Scott. 1994. Reflexivity and its Doubles: Structure, Aesthetics, and Community. In *Reflexive Modernization, Politics, Tradition and Aesthetics in the Modern Social Order*, eds. Ulrich Beck, Anthony Giddens, and Scott Lash. Stanford, CA: Stanford University Press.

Lee, Orville. 1998. Culture and Democratic Theory: Toward a Theory of Symbolic Democracy. *Constellations* 5 (4): 433–455.

Leet, Martin. 2004. *The Aftereffects of Knowledge in Modernity, Politics, Aesthetics and Individuality.* Albany: State University of New York Press.

Locke, John. 1990. *Treatise of Civil Government. On Locke, Berkeley, and Hume.* CD-ROM. Pittsboro, NC: Intelex Corporation.

Lont, Cynthia. 1984. Between Rock and a Hard Place: Subcultural Persistence and Women's Music. PhD diss., University of Iowa.

———. 1992. Women's Music: No Longer a Small Private Party. In *Rockin' the Boat: Mass Music and Mass*

Movements, ed. Reebee Garofalo. Boston: South End Press.

Lorde, Audre. 1984. *Sister Outsider: Essays and Speeches.* Freedom, CA: The Crossing Press.

Love, Nancy S. 1991. Politics and Voices: An Empowerment/ Knowledge Regime? *Differences: A Journal of Feminist Cultural Studies* 3 (Winter): 85–104.

———. 1999. Why Do the Sirens Sing? Figuring the Feminine in *Dialectic of Enlightenment. Theory and Event* 3 (1).

Lovell, John, Jr. 1972. *Black Song, The Forge and the Flame, The story of how the Afro-American Spiritual was hammered out.* New York: Paragon House Publishers.

Mattern, Mark. 1998. *Acting in Concert: Music, Community, and Political Action.* New Brunswick: Rutgers University Press.

McCarthy, Thomas. 1987. Introduction to *The Philosophical Discourse of Modernity.* Trans. Thomas McCarthy. Cambridge, MA: MIT Press.

———. 1994. Kantian Constructivism and Reconstructivism: Rawls and Habermas in Dialogue. *Ethics, an International Journal of Social, Political, and Legal Philosophy* 105:44–63.

McClary, Susan. 1993. Reshaping a Discipline: Musicology and Feminism in the 1990s. *Feminist Studies* 19 (2): 403–422.

McGinnis, Ann Cain. 1980. Music and Healing. *Heresies* 3 (2): 11–14.

McNeill, William H. 1995. *Keeping Together In Time, Dance and Drill in Human History.* Cambridge, MA: Harvard University Press.

Melucci, Alberto. 1996. *Challenging Codes: Collective Action in the Information Age.* New York: Cambridge University Press.

Mendieta, Eduardo. 2002. Introduction to *Religion and Rationality, Essays on Reason, God, and Modernity*. Ed. by Eduardo Mendieta. Cambridge, MA: 2002.

Mercosur Youth Orchestra. Retrieved 10 January 2003 from the World Wide Web. http://www.orquestamercosur.org/english.html.

Middleton, Richard. 2000. Introduction: Locating the Popular Music Text. In *Reading Pop, Approaches To Textual Analysis in Popular Music*, ed. Richard Middleton. Oxford: Oxford University Press.

Miller, Eugene F. 1979. Metaphor and Political Knowledge. *American Political Science Review* 73(1): 155–170.

Monson, Ingrid. 1996. *saying something, jazz improvisation and interaction.* Chicago: University of Illinois Press.

Morris, Martin. 2001. *Rethinking the Communicative Turn: Adorno, Habermas, and the Problem of Communicative Freedom.* Albany: State University of New York Press.

Moten, Fred. 2003. *In the Break, The Aesthetics of the Black Radical Tradition.* Minneapolis: University of Minnesota Press.

Nash, Alanna. 1988. Holly Near. *Stereo Review* 53 (1): 86–87.

———. 1991. Holly Near. *Stereo Review* 56 (1): 122.

Near, Holly. 1985. Smile beneath your tears: Women's Song and Resistance in Uruguay. In *Cultures in Contention,* ed. Douglas Kahn and Diane Neumaier. Seattle: Real Comet Press. 76–81.

———. © 1987. *Don't Hold Back,* Redwood Records RRCD 413, CD.

———. © 1989. *Sky Dances*, Redwood Records 8902, CD.

———. 1990. Grace Notes from Holly Near. *Ms.* (Nov./Dec.): 62.

Near, Holly, with Karen Conti. 1979. On Performing. *Paid My Dues: A Quarterly Journal of Women in Music.* 3 (3): 12–15, 41–44.

Near, Holly, with Derk Richardson. 1990. *Fire in the Rain Singer in the Storm: An Autobiography.* New York: William Morrow.

Nelson, John. 1998. *Tropes of Politics: Science, Theory, Rhetoric, Action.* Madison, WI: University of Wisconsin Press.

Odedoyin, Remi. 2000. Overlapping Consensus: Objectivising a Subjective Standpoint. *Journal of Philosophical Research* 25:323–343.

Ong, Walter. 1977. *Interfaces of the Word: Studies in the Evolution of Consciousness and Culture.* Ithaca: Cornell University Press.

———. 1991. *Orality and Literacy: The Technologizing of the Word.* New York: Routledge.

Osborne, William. 1994. Performer's Place. Art is Just an Excuse: Gender Bias in International Orchestras. *IAWM Journal* 2(3): 6–14.

———. 1999. Symphony Orchestras and Artist-Prophets: Cultural Isomorphism and the Allocation of Power in Music. *Leonardo Music Journal* (9): 69–76.

Pegley, Karen, and Virginia Caputo. 1994. Growing up Female(s): Retrospective Thoughts on Musical Preferences and Meanings. In *Queering the Pitch: The new gay and lesbian musicology.* New York: Routledge.

Philipson, Irene, and Omi, Michael. 1984. Singing for Their Lives: An interview with Holly Near and Ronnie Gilbert. *Socialist Review* 73 (Jan./Feb.): 79–92.

Pratt, Mary L. 1977. *Toward a Speech Act Theory of Literary Discourse.* Bloomington: Indiana University Press.

Pratt, Ray. 1994. *Rhythm and Resistance: The Political Uses of American Popular Music.* Washington, DC: Smithsonian Institution Press.

Rawls, John. 1955. Two Concepts of Rules. In *John Rawls: Collected Papers,* ed. Samuel Freeman. Cambridge, MA: Harvard University Press.

———. 1958. Justice as Fairness. In *John Rawls: Collected Papers,* ed. Samuel Freeman. Cambridge, MA: Harvard University Press.

———. 1971. Justice as Reciprocity. In *John Rawls: Collected Papers,* ed. Samuel Freeman. Cambridge, MA: Harvard University Press, 1999.

———. 1996. *Political Liberalism.* New York: Columbia University Press.

———. 1999a. *A Theory of Justice.* Rev. ed. New York: Columbia University Press.

———. 1999b. *The Law of Peoples: with, "the Idea of Public Reason Revisited."* Cambridge, MA: Harvard University Press.

Reagon, Bernice Johnson. 1980. *Songs of the Civil Rights Movement, 1955–1965: A Study in Culture History.* Ann Arbor, MI: University Microfilms.

———. 1983. Songs That Moved The Movement. *Perspectives: the Civil Rights Quarterly* (Summer): 27–35.

———. 1993a. "Let Your Light Shine"–Historical Notes. In *We Who Believe in Freedom: Sweet Honey in the Rock . . . Still on the Journey*, ed. Bernice Johnson Reagon and Sweet Honey in the Rock. New York: Doubleday.

———. 1993b. Singing For My Life. In *We Who Believe in Freedom: Sweet Honey in the Rock . . . Still on the Journey,* ed. Bernice Johnson Reagon and Sweet Honey in the Rock. New York: Doubleday.

———. 2001. *If You Don't Go, Don't Hinder Me, The African American Sacred Song Tradition.* Lincoln, NE: University of Nebraska Press.

Redfield, Marc. 2003. *The Politics of Aesthetics, Nationalism, Gender, Romanticism*. Stanford, CA: Stanford University Press.

Richardson, Derk. 1982. Holly Near's current tour aims to disarm. *In These Times*, 11 November, 13–14.

Riker, William H. 1983. Political Theory and the Art of Heresthetics. In *Political Science: The State of the Discipline,* ed. Ada W. Finifter. Washington, DC: The American Political Science Association.

Robbins, Bruce. 1990. Introduction: The Grounding of Intellectuals. In *Intellectuals, Aesthetics, Politics, Academics,* ed. Bruce Robbins. Minneapolis: University of Minnesota Press.

Robinson, Louise. 1993. Taking It To The Streets. In *Sweet Honey in the Rock . . . Still on the Journey*, ed. Bernice Johnson Reagon and Sweet Honey in the Rock. New York: Doubleday.

Rodnitzsky, Jerome. 1975. Songs of Sisterhood: The Music of Women's Liberation. *Popular Music and Society* IV (2): 77–85.

Rosen, Charles. 1997. *The Classical Style, Haydn, Mozart, Beethoven.* New York: W.W. Norton & Co.

Rothstein, Edward. 1986. The New Amateur Player and Listener. In *The Orchestra: Origins and Transformations*, ed. Joan Peyser. New York: Charles Scribner's Sons.

Rycenga, Jennifer. 1994. Lesbian Compositional Practices: One Lover-Composer's Perspective. In *Queering the Pitch: The new gay and lesbian musicology,* ed. Phillip Brett, Elizabeth Wood and Gary C. Thomas. New York: Routledge.

Salvaggio, Ruth. 1999. *The Sounds of Feminist Theory.* Albany: State University of New York Press.

Sanger, Kerran L. 1995. *"When the Spirit Says Sing": The Role of Freedom Songs in the Civil Rights Movement.* New York: Garland.

Schattschneider, E.E. 1975. *The Semi-Sovereign People, A Realist's View of Democracy in America.* Hinsdale, IL: Dryden Press.

Scheffler, Samuel. 1994. The Appeal of Political Liberalism. *Ethics, an International Journal of Social, Political, and Legal Philosophy* 105(1): 4–22.

Schoolman, Morton. 2001. *Reason and Horror: Critical Theory, Democracy, and Aesthetic Individuality.* New York: Routledge.

Schweickart, Patrocinio P. 1996. Speech Is Silver, Silence Is Gold: The Asymmetrical Intersubjectivity of Communicative Action. In *Knowledge, Difference, and Power: Essays Inspired by Women's Ways of Knowing.* Eds. Nancy Rule Goldberger, Jill M. Tarule, Blynche Clinchy, and Mary F. Belenky. New York: Basic Books.

Seeger, Pete and Bob Reiser, including many songs collected by Guy and Candie Carawan. 1989. *Everybody Says Freedom.* New York: W.W. Norton & Co.

Shepherd, John. 1993. Difference and Power in Music. In *Musicology and Difference: Gender and Sexuality in Music Scholarship,* ed. Ruth A. Solie. Berkeley: University of California Press.

Sheridan, Molly. 2000. American Sound Redefined, Composer Brent Michael Davids Brings A Native American Powwow Into the Concert Hall. *Symphony Magazine* (May-June). Retrieved January 30, 2003 from the World Wide Web http://www.brentmichaeldavids.com/writings-rev_amersound.htm

Shore, Bernard. 1938. *Orchestra Speaks.* Freeport, NY: Books for Libraries Press.

Silverman, Kaja. 1988. *The Acoustic Mirror: The Female Voice in Psychoanalysis and Cinema.* Bloomington: Indiana University Press.

"Sing To Me The Dream," from Holly Near's *Singer in the Storm*, Chameleon Music Group D274832, © 1990 CD. By Holly Hear and Jorge Coulon. Copyright 1984 Hereford Music (ASCAP).

"Singing For Our Lives" from Holly Near's *HARP: A Time to Sing*, Appleseed Records 1954, © 2001 CD. By Holly Near. 1979 Hereford Music (ASCAP).

"Sky Dances" from Holly Near's *Early Warnings*, Appleseed Records 1056, © 2001 CD. Words by Jimmy Durham. Music by Roy Brown. Copyright 1987 Discos Lara-Yari (ASCAP).

Slobin, Mark. 1993. *Subcultural Sounds: Micromusics of the West.* Hanover, NH: University Press of New England.

"Song To A Melody," from Holly Near's *You Can Know All I Am*, Redwood Records 3600. © 1976, Album. Words by Jeff Langley and Ginger Sarber. Music by Jeff Langley. © 1975 Hereford Music (ASCAP).

Spencer, John. 1996. *Re-Searching Black Music.* Knoxville: University of Tennessee Press.

Stevens, Dennis. 1986. Why Conductors? Their Role and the Idea of Fidelity. In *The Orchestra: Its Origin and Transformation.* New York: Charles Scribner's Sons.

Tambornino, John. 2000. *The Corporeal Turn.* New York: Routledge.

Tarrow, Sidney. 1998. *Power in Movement: Social Movements and Contentious Politics.* Cambridge, UK: Cambridge University Press.

Tilchen, Maida. 1984. Lesbians and Women's Music. In *Women-Identified Women.* Eds. Trudy Darty and Sandee Potter. Palo Alto, CA: Mayfield Publishing Co.

Tucker, Karen Iris. November 25, 2003. Still So Sweet. *The Advocate* 903: 64.

Van Gelder, Lindsay. 1985. Holly Near. *Ms.* 13 (7): 72–73

Verba, Sidney, Kay Lehman Schlozman, and Henry E. Brady. 1995. *Voice and Equality: Civic Voluntarism in American Politics.* Cambridge, MA: Harvard University Press.

Von Humboldt, Wilhelm. 1969. *The Limits of State Action.* Ed. J.W. Burrow. Cambridge, UK: Cambridge University Press.

Walker, Wyatt Tee. 1979. *"Somebody's Calling My Name": Black Sacred Music and Social Change.* Valley Forge, PA: Judson Press.

Walzer, Michael. 1994. Comment. In *Multiculturalism, Examining the Politics of Recognition*, ed. Amy Gutmann. Princeton, NJ: Princeton University Press.

Watrous, Susan, and Bob Blanchard. 1990. Holly Near: The Progressive Interview. *The Progressive.* 54 (3): 34–38.

Weiss, Michael D. 1993. A Jurisprudence of Blindness: Rawls' Justice and Legal Theory. *Drake Law Review* 42:565–589.

Wenar, Leif. 1995. Political Liberalism: An Internal Critique. *Ethics, an International Journal of Social, Political, and Legal Philosophy*. 106(1): 32–62.

White, Stephen K. 1991. *Political Theory and Postmodernism.* New York: Cambridge University Press.

———. 2000. *Sustaining Affirmation: The Strengths of Weak Ontology in Political Theory.* Princeton, NJ: Princeton University Press.

"You Bet," from Holly Near's *Simply Love: The Women's Music Collection*, Calico Tracks Music CTM0003, © 2000 CD. Words by Holly Near. Music by Meg Christian. Copyright 1978 Hereford Music/Thumbelina Music (ASCAP).

Young, Iris Marion. 1990. *Justice and the Politics of Difference.* Princeton, NJ: Princeton University Press.

———. 1997. *Intersecting Voices: Dilemmas of Gender, Political Philosophy, and Policy.* Princeton, NJ: Princeton University Press.

———. 2000. *Inclusion and Democracy.* New York: Oxford University Press.

Index